The Geography of Entrepreneurial Psychology

ENTREPRENEURSHIP FOOTPRINTS

Series Editor: Per Davidsson, *Director & Talbot Family Foundation Chair in Entrepreneurship, Australian Centre for Entrepreneurship Research (ACE) | QUT Business School (Management), Australia*

Presenting a new series of short books defining the future of entrepreneurship research. Leading thinkers are given the space to build on their contribution to entrepreneurship to give the reader a concise, innovative and 'must-read, must-cite' take on entrepreneurship research.

More in depth than a journal article, shorter than a standard book and refreshing to read, these books will be the starting point for future research in a particular sub-field for both new and established academics.

Titles in the series include:

Entrepreneurial Ecosystems
Theory, Practice and Futures
Ben Spigel

The Profits and Perils of Passion in Entrepreneurship
Stoking the Fires and Banking the Coals
Melissa S. Cardon and Charles Y. Murnieks

The Geography of Entrepreneurial Psychology
Martin Obschonka, Michael Fritsch and Michael Stuetzer

The Geography
of Entrepreneurial
Psychology

Martin Obschonka

Professor in Entrepreneurship, Australian Centre for Entrepreneurship Research, Queensland University of Technology, Australia

Michael Fritsch

Professor of Economics, School of Economics and Business Administration, Friedrich Schiller University Jena, Germany

Michael Stuetzer

Professor of Economics and Quantitative Methods, Cooperative State University Baden-Wuerttemberg, Germany

ENTREPRENEURSHIP FOOTPRINTS

 Edward Elgar
PUBLISHING

Cheltenham, UK • Northampton, MA, USA

Published by
Edward Elgar Publishing Limited
The Lypiatts
15 Lansdown Road
Cheltenham
Glos GL50 2JA
UK

Edward Elgar Publishing, Inc.
William Pratt House
9 Dewey Court
Northampton
Massachusetts 01060
USA

A catalogue record for this book
is available from the British Library

Library of Congress Control Number: 2021935860

This book is available electronically in the **Elgar**online
Business subject collection
http://dx.doi.org/10.4337/9781788973380

ISBN 978 1 78897 337 3 (cased)
ISBN 978 1 78897 338 0 (eBook)

Printed and bound in Great Britain by TJ Books Limited, Padstow, Cornwall

Contents

v

Figures

1. Entrepreneurship and psychology in geographic context: introduction

1.1 BACKGROUND

A vivid start-up culture – this is the common response one hears around the globe today when discussing key goals for regional development with policymakers, educators, business leaders, venture capitalists and entrepreneurs. While often cited examples for particularly successful start-up hubs are Silicon Valley and the Bay Area, Tel Aviv, London, Bangalore, Berlin and São Paulo, a vivid start-up culture is not only on the policy agenda of megacities and economic powerhouses; it represents an omnipresent policy target for all kinds of regions, cities and places (OECD 2020). But what is a vivid start-up culture? What are its key components? Can it be developed or is it simply a by-product of regional wealth and economic characteristics? And what is the people side of a vivid start-up culture? This book is devoted to these questions. Specifically, it attempts to make a contribution by addressing these questions from the perspective of geographical psychology. The existing research evidence, and the variety of new implications for entrepreneurship research, practice and policy, give rise to the foundation and definition of a new interdisciplinary research field – the geography of entrepreneurial psychology. This book gives an overview of the current state of this research and its implications.

What is entrepreneurship? The many definitions often have a common core – behaviors such as being proactive, taking risks and creating something new, often motivated by a desire of self-realization and autonomy. While such behaviors can be found in all kinds of organizational contexts, most of the empirical research on entrepreneurship focuses on the formation of new businesses, which can be an important driver of economic development (Davidsson 2016b; Fritsch 2013; OECD 2020).

Because entrepreneurship is about certain behaviors, psychology as an academic discipline plays a key role – together with economics, management, sociology and geography – to name just the main disciplines involved in the interdisciplinary endeavor that is contemporary entrepreneurship research (Landström 2020). Economics, management and sociology deal particularly with incentives for different kinds of entrepreneurship and its effects. Geography is involved because regional conditions and dynamics drive various kinds of economic activities and outcomes (Fujita and Krugman 2004). This includes entrepreneurship, which is also regarded as a "regional event" (Feldman 2001) – something that is enabled by the interplay between different local factors in a given place or region (OECD 2020).

1.2   ENTREPRENEURSHIP ACROSS SPACE

Taking new business formation as an indicator of entrepreneurship, the number of start-ups or of people who are involved in the creation of a new venture shows tremendous geographical variation. There are sizeable differences in the levels of entrepreneurship across countries and such differences are even larger between the regions or places within a country. Variation of entrepreneurship across countries can have many reasons such as respective differences in formal institutions that tend to apply nationwide, whereas the determinants of regional differences within a country are more place-specific. Quite regularly, the variation of these regional conditions within countries is considerably larger than their variation between countries, indicating their important role.

Cities as a regional unit deserve special attention (Glaeser 2011). City size and population density represent a diversity of important influences on entrepreneurship such as availability of inputs (e.g., labor and finance), proximity to competitors on input and output markets, as well as price levels. Since R&D activities of private firms, universities and other public research institutions tend to be located in larger cities, number of population and density in a region also indicate the availability of knowledge spillovers. Density is, however, also closely related to agglomeration diseconomies such as congestion, high cost of living, unfavorable environmental conditions and crime (Sternberg 2009).

Recent research has also identified an important role of a region's history on its level of entrepreneurship (Fritsch and Wyrwich 2019; Glaeser et al. 2015). The empirical evidence suggests that a region's history can lead to certain informal institutions (North 1994; Williamson 2000) that tend to be long-lasting. Due to such effects of historical factors, regions tend to follow specific development trajectories.

Economists and economic geographers have made a distinction between hard and soft factors that may contribute to the observed geographic heterogeneity in entrepreneurial activity and to the developmental trajectories of regions. The hard factors, which are relatively easy to measure, comprise, for example, the legal framework and public policy, age structure and qualification of the workforce, industry structure and density of economic activities (Bosma 2013; Sternberg 2009). Particularly important effects on regional entrepreneurial activity have been found for the size structure and the industry structure of the local economy. Based on the empirical finding that the largest share of founders has worked in small (vs. larger) firms before starting an own venture, the small firm sector is characterized as a seedbed for regional entrepreneurship (Fritsch and Falck 2007; Parker 2004). While regions with a large employment share in small firms tend to have relatively many start-ups, the opposite is found for places that are dominated by large-scale industries such as mining and steel (Stuetzer et al. 2016). Industry structure influences the qualifications and skills of the regional population that can affect entrepreneurial intentions and the prospects of start-ups.

While information on hard factors is often provided by official statistics, soft factors are more or less guesswork (Marshall 1920) so that their measurement is difficult and often incomplete. Many economists and economic geographers agree, however, that soft factors are particularly important for entrepreneurship, making them a promising and interesting research subject (Audretsch et al. 2019; Fritsch and Storey 2014; Saxenian 1996). There is, however, no consensus on how one can conceptualize and measure them. The respective literature often uses relatively loosely defined terms for the description of soft factors such as culture, history and traditions, or regional images. However, these terms may not deliver sufficiently concrete implications for entrepreneurship research and practice, or for public policy aiming to develop regional entrepreneurship.

Hence, while empirical research has resulted in a solid set of hard factors that tend to influence entrepreneurship in terms of new business formation, the effect of the soft factors is much less clear. In fact, the systematic investigation of relevant soft factors has become one of the major research goals in contemporary economics and economic geography. For example, while many experts seem to agree that local culture is important for regional entrepreneurship (e.g., OECD 2020), the term is extremely abstract and non-tangible – a black box for researchers, practitioners and policymakers alike.

So how can one investigate soft factors systematically, if they are that important? Most research in this field seems to agree that it is important to understand *the people side* of local mechanisms driving entrepreneurship. Among the different approaches from various disciplines that offer systematic concepts and analytical frameworks for investigating this people side, geographical psychology has become a promising and fruitful scholarly lens to conceptualize and measure some of the soft factors behind regional entrepreneurship.

In the following, we give a brief overview over the field of geographical psychology and how it is imbedded in the wider discipline of psychology.

1.3   CONNECTING SPACE AND PSYCHOLOGY: GEOGRAPHICAL PSYCHOLOGY

While psychological science has a traditional focus on intra-psychic processes (by examining what many in the wider public would typically regard as "psychological"), there is also a remarkably strong interest in context in contemporary psychological science. Relevant contexts can be very proximal to the individual (e.g., the immediate social and physical environment with which the individual directly interacts on a regular basis, such as the social and physical components of the family, friends/peers, work and leisure contexts). Other relevant contexts that are more distal to the individual, such as local and national institutions, also matter, often by shaping the more proximal contexts.

Across the life-span, people are situated in, and interact with, various contexts and levels of contexts, which can interact with others and change over time (Bronfenbrenner 1979). For example, people are selected into contexts (e.g., as function of normative age-correlated processes or of historical influences and changes in the macro-context) (Baltes et al. 2007). But people are not just passive; they are also active agents in their own development (Bandura et al. 1999), for example by proactively selecting, using and shaping contexts (Baltes and Baltes 2014; Lerner 1982).

Even biological perspectives in psychology (e.g., behavioral genetics; see Plomin et al. 2003) take context very seriously, not only because people with their dispositions interact with the environment and many psychosocial outcomes can be understood as a product of gene–environment interactions (Moffitt et al. 2005; Ullen et al. 2016), but also because the environment can even affect biological levels of mind and behavior in a deeper way (Gottlieb 2003). For example, advances in the field of epigenetics have demonstrated that environmental and psychosocial factors can change the epigenome, and some studies have even showed that this can also be potentially transmitted to more than one generation of descendants. Hence, the environment has the potential to change the effect of genes (e.g., their expression in mind and behavior) not just for one generation, but for future descendant generations that might no longer be exposed to this environment (Jones et al. 2018; Masterpasqua 2009).

It is thus almost impossible to separate biology and environment in psychology (Rutter 2006). In other words, if biology (e.g., genes) is an essential component of mind and behavior, this also applies to the environment, and particularly to the interaction and transaction between biology and the environment, often mediated via human agency. This makes clear that a context-minded perspective matters to virtually all topics and fields of psychology. Psychological sciences have thus benefited from overlap and interdisciplinary exchange with adjacent fields such as sociology and biological ecology. Another field that is a less obvious partner for psychological research interested in context is human geography (Fouberg and Murphy 2020; Gregory and Walford 2016).

The scholarly field of human geography studies the interrelations between people, place and environment, considering particularly spatial and temporal factors of locations. Whereas physical geography focuses more on spatial aspects and mechanisms of the natural world, human geography is more interested in people, and the spatial organization and processes shaping their interactions with social and physical contexts. Ideas and insights from human geography have inspired and informed psychological science in a way that we have witnessed the emergence of the new subfield of geographical psychology, which is explicitly embracing the geographical perspective.

Broadly speaking, a geographical perspective to psychology applies a context perspective to psychology by taking the objective nature of the context seriously (instead of mere personal perceptions) – the geographical feature of the context itself, e.g., what defines a place or a region in terms of space. It is thus very different from inward-looking psychological science that emphasizes subjective perceptions and intrapsychic processes, e.g., how people think and decide. Geographical psychology is embedded in socioecological perspectives in psychology (see Oishi and Graham 2010), where the broader focus is on social ecology comprised of both physical and human environments.

Rentfrow and Jokela (2016) define geographical psychology as a research field that "aims to integrate psychology and the different levels of geographic analysis by focusing on the spatial distribution of psychological phenomena and their relations to features of the macro environment" (p. 393). Importantly, they see geographical psychology as linked yet independent of cross-cultural psychology. They stress that "both are concerned with connections between psychological phenomena and the broader environment" (p. 393), but "cross-cultural psychology focuses on connections between psychological phenomena and cultural symbols, practices, and norms without focusing specifically on geographic distributions" (p. 393). In contrast, "geographical psychology seeks to discover and understand the spatial organization of psychological phenomena and how that organization relates to individual behavior and the macro environment" (p. 393). Hence, geographical psychology puts a strong focus on a spatial component – how psychological factors and mechanisms (human behaviors and mindsets) vary and function across places and regions, as well as within and across *different* regional levels more broadly. This geographic component is fundamental, for example, in economic geography.

1.4 THE GEOGRAPHY OF ENTREPRENEURIAL PSYCHOLOGY: A DEFINITION

Drawing from the definition of geographical psychology (Rentfrow and Jokela 2016), the field of the geography of entrepreneurial psychology can be defined as *the scholarly examination of the spatial organization of psychological phenomena associated with entrepreneurship*. The research field is therefore located at the intersection between psychology, geography, economics and sociology. It puts a special focus on perspectives in geographical psychology and economic geography.

The field uses concepts, constructs and empirical insights from micro-level psychology (e.g., individual-level personality research) to develop and measure concepts and constructs at the aggregate geographical level. The micro-foundations of the macro-level focus in the geography of entrepreneurial psychology draw from various subdisciplines of psychology such as personality psychology, social psychology, work psychology/organization behavior, developmental psychology, biological psychology, health psychology and cognitive psychology. The field also integrates various approaches from economics and economic geography (e.g., spatial economic dynamics, cultural economics and economic history).

Starting with micro-level theories and concepts to understand and examine a macro-level phenomenon is not only a common strategy in geographical psychology (Rentfrow and Jokela 2016) but also in economics. In fact, the core of an economic approach to the social sciences is at the micro-level of individual behavior (Becker 1976; Kirchgässner 2008).

Economics regards this individual behavior as the result of rational decisions based on utility considerations and commonly applies these micro-level theories to the explanation to aggregate behavior at the macro-level (e.g., consumption theory, theory of investment). The central idea of this individualistic method is that all macro-phenomena can be traced back to micro-behavior so that there is no basic ontological difference between these two levels.

It is also important to note that the field of the geography of entrepreneurial psychology overlaps with perspectives in culture research in entrepreneurship (Beugelsdijk and Smeets 2008; Davidsson 1995; Hayton and Cacciotti 2013; Stephan and Uhlaner 2010). However, it is different from cross-cultural psychological approaches insofar as "cross-cultural psychology focuses on connections between psychological phenomena and cultural symbols, practices, and norms without focusing specifically on spatial distributions (Oishi and Graham 2010; Rozin 2003). In contrast, geographical psychology seeks to discover and understand the spatial organization of psychological phenomena and how that organization relates to individual behavior and the macro environment" (Rentfrow and Jokela 2016, p. 393). Hence, research on the geography of entrepreneurial psychology can contribute to our understanding of an entrepreneurial culture but it should not be equated with culture research (Hofstede and McCrae 2004).

1.5   PURPOSE OF THE BOOK

This book provides an introduction into the geography of entrepreneurial psychology as an emerging field of research. Chapter 2 gives an overview of the micro-level psychology of entrepreneurship that provides the micro-foundations of the geography of entrepreneurial psychology. Chapter 3 then turns to empirical work on the macro-phenomenon of the psychology of entrepreneurship – the geographic variation of psychological factors associated with entrepreneurship. In Chapter 4 we discuss the phenomenon of regional levels of new venture creation and self-employment that have often been found to be rather persistent over long periods of time despite disruptive events such as devastating wars, several decades of socialist regime that followed anti-entrepreneurial policies, or even a nearly complete exchange of the local population. This in turn has important implications for the geography of entrepreneurial psychology and vice versa.

Chapter 5 surveys research on historical origins of regional differences in regional psychological factors, including the historical local exploitation of natural resources, as well as historical political and economic institutions. Chapter 6 discusses implications for practice, education and policy, and Chapter 7 proposes an extended agenda for future research on the topic. Chapter 8 provides a final summary and outlook.

2. Micro-level psychology of entrepreneurship

2.1 BACKGROUND

Psychology is a popular research discipline in the social sciences, with manifold implications for the wider public and society in general. Its history as an emancipated, independent scholarly field reaches back to the late nineteenth century when Wilhelm Wundt founded the first psychological laboratory in the city of Leipzig, Germany. This had established a strong empirical focus in the field (Wundt 1874), valuing the scientific method, and thus research rigor and relevance (Benjamin 2018). Since then, psychology has evolved into a highly complex research field spanning basic research (e.g., on perception, memory, cognition, personality, genetics and decision-making) and applied research (e.g., clinical psychology, industrial and organizational psychology, educational psychology, media psychology and economic psychology). This relatively broad conceptualization of modern psychology as a scholarly field is also reflected in its current self-understanding. For example, stressing the scope of contemporary psychological research, the American Psychological Association defines psychology as the following:

> Psychology is the study of the mind and behavior. The discipline embraces all aspects of the human experience—from the functions of the brain to the actions of nations, from child development to care for the aged. In every conceivable setting from scientific research centers to mental healthcare services,

"the understanding of behavior" is the enterprise of psychologists.
(https://www.apa.org/support/about-apa; retrieved July 20, 2020)

With its focus on understanding human behavior and underlying mental processes, psychology is bound to contribute to the scholarly field of entrepreneurship. This is because entrepreneurship requires human agency. Ultimately, businesses are started by individuals (at least until a new era of advanced AI might replace entrepreneurs; see Obschonka and Audretsch 2020). The study of the psychology of entrepreneurship can thus be seen as a prototypical example of applied psychological research interested in a relevant type of real-world behavior – relevant for individual careers, but also for society in terms of technological and economic progress (Audretsch and Thurik 2001).

As in many applied research fields studying human behavior, psychological theories, concepts and mechanisms are also a popular research focus in the field of entrepreneurship research (Frese 2009; Gorgievski and Stephan 2016; Hisrich et al. 2007). With the explosion of entrepreneurship research in terms of scope of topics and volume of studies and publications since the 1990s, the study of psychological aspects and mechanisms associated with entrepreneurial behavior has also expanded rapidly. Psychological perspectives can be found, for example, in research at the micro-level (e.g., the characteristics, mental processes and behaviors of the entrepreneur), at the organizational level (e.g., on entrepreneurial teams) and also at the macro-level (e.g., when studying entrepreneurial regions and country comparisons). Put differently, psychological perspectives have been proven useful to study entrepreneurship at all relevant levels – individual, team and organization, as well as region and country.

Psychological science offers a rich toolbox for entrepreneurship researchers, with respect to concepts and theories as well as research perspectives and methods (Davidsson 2016a). Indeed, insights and methods from many subfields of basic and applied psychology have been applied and tested in entrepreneurship research. For example, when focusing on the single individual, the psychology of entrepreneurship is interested in the entrepreneurial mindset and entrepreneurial behavior. This can involve biological, agentic/behavioral, developmental and contextual levels of human functioning as well as their interactions and transactions over time. Today, such research reaches, for example, from the genetics of entrepreneurship (e.g., Nicolaou et al. 2008), to personal agency (e.g., Frese 2009; McMullen et al. 2020; Newman et al. 2019), to the development of the entrepreneurial mindset over the life-span (e.g., Gielnik et al. 2018; Obschonka 2016). Research in the psychology of entrepreneurship can also be conducted at various context levels such as regions (e.g., Obschonka et al. 2013) and countries (Stephan and Uhlaner 2010), focusing on its effects and roots. Taken together, the psychology of entrepreneurship fulfills the broader promise of psychology as a discipline that can embrace all aspects of the human experience.

In stark contrast to this popularity and broad scope of psychologically informed entrepreneurship research, and the various insights it has been delivering to a better understanding of entrepreneurship, the usefulness of psychological perspectives is not without criticism in the field. For example, some entrepreneurship scholars reiterate that one should not look so much at personal characteristics (e.g., mindset) but instead solely at what entrepreneurs actually do as independent of their psychological factors and mainly driven by situational and contextual factors – a notion that would imply that psychological approaches for understanding entrepreneurial behavior, and thus entrepreneurship, are in general misleading (Gartner 1988; Ramoglou et al. 2020).

Nevertheless, many entrepreneurship scholars would agree that when applying psychology to entrepreneurship research and practice, it has a clear potential to make important contributions to progress in both the scholarly field and the real-world phenomenon. Psychology has a long history of informing practice and policymakers (e.g., Antonakis 2017; Bleidorn et al. 2019) and many entrepreneurship scholars have embraced psychology to deliver concrete practical implications for the field of entrepreneurship. This seems to be more important than ever, as Wiklund, Wright and Zahra (2019) recently defined (better and more visible) research relevance as entrepreneurship research's current grand challenge.

Excluding the psychological component from entrepreneurship reminds us about a related expulsion in the field of economics. Economists are interested in firm behavior in markets, regarding their decisions about prices, quantities, investments in new machines and equipment, producing high or low quality products, and so on. Driven by the ideals of rigor in the natural sciences, these decisions have been modeled increasingly with mathematical equations and the motivation of the firms have become narrowly restricted to maximizing profits or minimizing costs. This approach ignored the human agency of firm leadership which is in most firms the entrepreneur and founder alone. Baumol (1968, p. 67) described this as if "the Prince of Denmark has been expunged from the discussion of Hamlet". For more than 50 years, few economists wrote about the entrepreneur and entrepreneurship. Only in recent decades has the entrepreneur made a comeback to economics as it has become increasingly clear that contemporary growth in employment, GDP and innovation are driven by start-ups and small firms (Acs and Audretsch 1988; Birch 1979; Lee 2017).

2.2 DIFFERENT CONCEPTUAL PERSPECTIVES AND PARADIGMS IN PSYCHOLOGICAL ENTREPRENEURSHIP RESEARCH

Over the more than 120 years of its history as an independent scholarly field, psychology has developed numerous theories, paradigms and research frameworks. This makes it basically impossible to review its full intellectual, empirical and social structure here, and it is clear that a concept like psychology of entrepreneurship has to focus on a few particularly influential and useful perspectives in psychology. However, this should not come at the expense of denying the existence of underlying paradigms, deeper debates and social structures. Indeed, some key approaches from the broad and diverse psychology field appear to be particularly useful for the current endeavor of defining the geography of entrepreneurial psychology. However, before we discuss these approaches, we would like to highlight a recent reflection of the social structure in contemporary entrepreneurship research as a scholarly field to position these approaches and underlying paradigms more adequately in the dynamics of contemporary entrepreneurship research and its community.

In a very interesting large-scale analysis of entrepreneurship scholars' perceptions about their research community and networks, Landström and Harirchi (2018) presented data indicating that entrepreneurship is a rather phenomena-driven research field, bound together by a shared communication system and social interaction. There is not a single core and narrow theoretical approach, but rather a diverse set of theoretical underpinnings. While early doubts of the legitimacy of entrepreneurship as a separate research field have vanished, it is still difficult to argue that entrepreneurship has developed into a larger coherent scholarly community. Landström and Harirchi (2018) present survey data from 3,000+ entrepreneurship researchers. Asked about their scholarly inspiration, the respondents named 414 different scholars. Thus, the field of entrepreneurship is characterized by a very diverse set of schools of thought and intellectual inspirations. This makes entrepreneurship different from other social sciences that are rather theory-driven and have a less diverse set of theoretical approaches, schools of thought and inspirational sources.

There are various possible reasons for this diversity. Firstly, theoretical underpinnings in entrepreneurship are often rooted

in related disciplines such as economics, sociology, management and psychology. A second and related argument is that
a large share of the main inspirational sources in entrepreneurship have received their academic training in an adjacent field.
What connects, for example, William Gartner, Per Davisson,
Michael Frese and Howard Aldrich is their common interest
in the real-word phenomenon of people thinking and acting
entrepreneurial. A third potential reason for this fragmen-
tation is that entrepreneurship has various manifestations.
There exist several dependent variables ranging from emotions, intentions, actions and outcomes in various settings
such as academia, new firms and employees, at various
levels such as the individual, team, networks and geographic
units (Davidsson 2016b). As in any large and fragmented
family, a research field needs hubs and meeting points.
Conferences such as the Annual Meeting of the Academy
of Management and the Babson College Entrepreneurship
Research Conference as well as multidisciplinary journals like
Journal of Business Venturing and *Small Business Economics*
have occupied this role (Landström and Harirchi 2018). To
a smaller extent, some entrepreneurship faculties that bring
together scholars from different fields have also emerged.

The above description of the social structure of contemporary entrepreneurship research is of direct relevance for
the current work that seeks to discuss and frame the paradigms and intellectual schools and origins relevant for the
geography of entrepreneurial psychology. One illustrative
example of how paradigm- and school-of-thought-driven
other fields differ from entrepreneurship is the fundamental
question in economics of how knowledge spillovers lead
to economic growth in agglomeration economies and why.
Various definitions and approaches exist, and major and
often cited empirical studies have attempted to test these
major approaches against each other (e.g., Glaeser et al.
1992; see also Caragliu, de Dominicis and de Groot 2016).
In contemporary entrepreneurship research, paradigms and

schools of thought are obviously less central or at least less highlighted in research publications and less influential in scholars' collective academic self-identity as entrepreneurship researchers. Interestingly, this could also help to explain why some scholars have criticized a too strong reliance on incremental theories, and incremental empirical contributions, in entrepreneurship research (Shepherd 2015; see also Tourish 2019). On the other hand, it is also clear that a stronger focus on real-world phenomena in the research field, and less paradigm-heavy conflicts and debates, also comes with various advantages for a growing and evolving research field and community (Davidsson 2016b).

Nevertheless, when defining a subfield in entrepreneurship research, like the geography of entrepreneurial psychology, it might be actually quite useful to make implicit paradigms and schools of thought more explicit to explicate the intellectual and empirical structure of the field. In this case, this concerns paradigms and schools of thought in psychology: What actually *is* the psychology of entrepreneurship? What is it *exactly* that can have a geographical component relevant for the broader field of entrepreneurship research and practice?

2.3 THE ACTION-ORIENTED PARADIGM

Without a doubt, the most influential psychologist in contemporary entrepreneurship research is Michael Frese. Any discussion of paradigms and schools of thought in the psychology of entrepreneurship would be incomplete if it did not highlight and integrate Frese's perspective and work.

Defining an action-oriented paradigm, Frese puts single actions at the center of his approach to a psychology of entrepreneurship (Frese 2009; Frese and Gielnik 2014). In his view, these actions are the central mediator between all psychological characteristics and traits, on the one hand, and tangible entrepreneurial outcomes, on the other. In other words, this paradigm argues that a psychology of entrepreneurship is first and foremost about actions (Frese 2009). Particularly important concepts in this psychology of action perspective are effort and personal initiative as they are the fuel of actions (Fay and Frese 2001). As people take action in a persistent manner, they are making things happen (Frese et al. 2007).

This action-oriented paradigm with its emphasis on the direct determinants of such actions such as effort and personal initiative is arguably particularly attractive from an intervention perspective. Intervention programs can be designed to stimulate entrepreneurial outcomes via training and reinforcing actions that directly lead to entrepreneurial outcomes (Campos et al. 2017). From a perspective of entrepreneurial outcomes, it is obviously far easier and more feasible to evoke effort and personal initiative that directly lead to these outcomes, than to change personality, underlying motivation patterns or other human attributes which are all more distal predictors of entrepreneurship itself. Interestingly, there is growing evidence that effort and personal initiative training can even shape deeper personality factors associated with entrepreneurship (e.g., Gielnik et al. 2015). That effort and proactive engagement itself can change personality is something that Frese had highlighted as early as 1982 as an influential yet under-researched occupational socialization process that shapes mindsets (Frese 1982).

What are the underlying paradigms and schools of thought behind Frese's influential action-oriented approach to entrepreneurship psychology? While we acknowledge that we can only *attempt* to provide a brief summary here, based on the existing literature, it is probably fair to draw the following picture. Before researching entrepreneurship, Frese already was an influential psychologist in the broader field of industrial and organizational psychology (also termed work psychology). The field of work psychology typically addresses behavioral outcomes in working individuals, but also the individual mindsets and psychosocial functioning and adaptation of these individuals. Frese's theoretical and empirical contributions to this field were to put "action as the core of work psychology" (Frese and Zapf 1994, p. 271). Action was thereby defined as goal-oriented behavior, as an expression of a concious goal. Prior to Frese, the field of work psychology in the 1950s and 1960s was more interested in motivation and abilities. In this action-focused paradigm, cognitions regulate actions within an enviromental input – a behavior nexus. This was not entirely new but based on seminal works of action-oriented theorizing and research in the social sciences, including research and approaches on the cognitive factors of action-regulation in context (e.g., Hacker 1998; Leontiev 1978, 1981; Miller et al. 1960). A recent, detailed overview over the foundations of this approach can be found in Zacher and Frese (2018).

Such an action-focused paradigm for work psychology implied, in its intellectual radicality, a distinct set of concepts and thought patterns. For example, in Frese's action regulation theory an action is broken down into a cycle of prototypical action sequences: (1) goals/redefinition of tasks, (2) information collection and prognosis, (3) plan and execution, and (4) monitoring and feedback (Frese 2009). Hence, planning and goal-setting are central (Miller et al. 1960), in addition to the essential behavioral components and a feedback component (Hacker 1998). In other words, in this view, literally any work behavior and thus work performance can be seen as cycles of such action sequences – and more broadly as the psychological regulation of concrete actions. Defining human nature as deeply mastery oriented (Frese 2009), this perspective basically asks why and how individuals take action in the work context in a successful way that proves a sense of control, that energizes them and their environment, and how this is regulated via psychological mechanisms that lend themselves to intervention and training. This action-orientation can also be applied to other contexts outside of the world of work, for example to the question of an active, successful ageing (Zacher et al. 2016) and later on entrepreneurship.

Another perspective implied by the action-oriented paradigm is the idea that it is not so much distant personality characteristics that shape work behaviors and work outcomes, but that work behavior itself, its associated actions and underlying cognitive processes can shape personality (Frese 1982). Hence, personality traits are not so much seen as a given and influential for the individual's work outcomes, but again actions are the center of interest as a causal agent not only for effects in the environment (e.g., work behaviors and performance) but also for deeper effects on the individual themself (Frese 2009; Frese et al. 2007). This occupational socialization perspective has added an action-oriented cognitive view to the broader intellectual debate in the social sciences on the deeper socializing effect of work on the individual (Kohn and Schooler 1973, 1982; Marx 1859). Again, history has confirmed Frese's visionary statement in 1982 that occupational socialization is under-researched yet a very promising and potential influential study subject (Frese et al. 1996). Indeed, since then, many studies have shown that work tasks and experiences, and associated agentic cognitive processes, can indeed shape personality to a certain degree (Frese et al. 2007; Roberts et al. 2003; Roberts and Mroczek 2008). However, it seems that selection processes (traits are the causal agents that shape people's careers and work behaviors; see Schneider et al. 1995) and socialization processes (work itself is the causal agent that shapes personality) also often interact with each other in a systematic way. Thus, if one wants to answer the question why individuals within an occupation, job or organization may sometimes be relatively similar to each other in terms of their personality or a single trait, the answer is that it can be a product of selection processes or a product of socialization processes, or both.

To conclude, the parsimonious "psycho-engineering" of concrete, structured psychological processes around single actions that are the central gear in the psychology of the working individual in Frese's approach is a masterpiece from an intellectual scholarly perspective. The paradigm of looking at actions and the cognitive regulation of these actions has left a deep mark in work psychology and in recent years particularly in entrepreneurship research. It resonates well with the view of some scholars that entrepreneurship research should not look so much at the entrepreneur as a person but at what entrepreneurs actually do (Gartner 1988; Ramoglou et al. 2020).

What are the implications of Frese's action-oriented paradigm for the geography of entrepreneurship psychology? A consistent progression would be to conceive a geography of entrepreneurial psychology as a geography of entrepreneurial actions and underlying cognitive regulation. Research questions would include how, why and under which conditions people in different regions differ in actions, effort and personal initiative. We believe that it is an important perspective. We also believe, however, that other paradigms and perspectives are useful as well, and that there can be a coexistence and integration of paradigms in the geography of entrepreneurial psychology.

In the following, for the sake of simplicity and clarity, we compare the action-oriented definition of entrepreneurial psychology to a person-oriented definition that highlights more the holistic nature of a person's personality. This includes a person's developmental history by placing the developing individual in the center of scientific inquiry, instead of concrete entrepreneurial actions. We acknowledge that this action-centric vs. person-centric world view dichotomy in the psychology of entrepreneurship is a very reductionist comparison. Both paradigms show partial overlap as, for example, both look at actions *and* personality traits and both emphasize the agentic role of the individual. However, the person-centric and action-centric paradigms approach things from rather different points of view, which is probably a more fundamental difference than one would think at first glance.

2.4   THE PERSON-ORIENTED PARADIGM

The person-oriented paradigm is based on the individual and is closely related to the broader field of personality psychology. This is a subfield of psychology that studies inter-individual differences such as traits and the personality of an individual as a dynamic, organized set of personal characteristics, and the behavior, motivation, cognitions and emotions of the person. Hence, if psychology can be defined as the study of the mind and behavior, this person-centric perspective might highlight the role of the mindset more than the primacy of actions and behaviors. Whereas the action-oriented perspective may see the individual as a tool in the toolbox of actions (e.g., how actions can have an effect on individuals and the environment), the person-oriented perspective sees actions as a tool in the toolbox of the individual (e.g., to express one's personality, to develop a life narrative and to reinforce a sense of identity and coherence) (see Davidsson 2007).

With this focus on the developing individual as embedded in a life course with changing developmental contexts, one can ask the question how the field of personality psychology can help to better understand an entrepreneurial personality from a holistic perspective interested in the person as a whole, in individuality and in personal agency motivated and guided not so much by single actions but by the person themself, a perspective that goes beyond a strict focus on the work context.

This study of personality traits has long roots in entrepreneurship research. Seminal theorizing by Knight (1921), McClelland (1961) and Schumpeter (1934) had placed the psychological nature of the entrepreneur in the center of the scientific debate around entrepreneurial behavior and its drivers. Recently, we have seen a renaissance of studies in this field (e.g., Kerr et al. 2018), with an increasingly elaborated focus on different types of traits (e.g., "bright" and "dark" traits, broad vs. specific traits, higher-order traits vs. sub-facets of higher order traits). However, what we have seen much less often in conceptual and empirical work is an analysis of the personality as a whole in the context of entrepreneurship. Obschonka and Stuetzer (2017, p. 204) use the following example to illustrate this point:

> ... let's assume the entrepreneurial mindset is comparable to a sheet of music for a complex piano sonata. Understandably, focusing on single components and notes of the sheet of music won't make it possible to understand the melody and structure of the sonata as a whole. Only if we look at the specific structure of all notes and their dynamics (e.g., how they relate to each other) can we understand the gestalt of the sonata, because the whole is clearly more than just the simple sum of its parts here. We believe that this gestalt perspective is indeed useful to understand the entrepreneurial mindset, which has important implications for research and practice.

An important motivation of this person-oriented perspective is to understand the individual as gestalt, the dynamic constellation of traits and other personal characteristics that together are more than the mere sum of the traits. Even more importantly, such within-person dynamics (e.g., efforts to maintain personality coherence; see Cervone and Shoda 1999; Sheldon and Kasser 1995) could motivate and guide behavior, in addition to the effect of the traits. In other words, a focus on personality is truly something different (and far more person-oriented) than a focus on traits. Such a focus on the gestalt of an individual's personality is reminiscent of the general desire in psychology to understand the individual as a whole. This holistic person-oriented perspective was established by Gordon Allport (1923), one of the fathers of personality psychology, who stressed: "More fundamental than differential psychology [i.e., the psychometric focus on dimensions of difference among people], by far, is the problem of the nature, the activity, and the unity of the *total personality*" (p. 614; original emphasis). This is a reminder that from a person-oriented perspective on the psychology of entrepreneurship, scholars should also try to understand the intra-individual psychological reality of individuals (Magnusson and Törestad 1993; McAdams and Pals 2006).

Hence, it is useful to understand personality as a system. This requires not only consideration of a broader set of traits and other personality characteristics to understand the personality of a person as a coherent whole, but also a focus on intra-individual dynamics between these single components of the personality system (Cervone and Shoda 1999; Sheldon and Kasser 1995). What maintains this system? How is it expressed in behaviors? At first glance these questions seem to be not directly related to the specific topic of entrepreneurship. However, as soon as one wants to understand the entrepreneurial mindset it might be useful to consider this person-oriented paradigm, in addition to the action-oriented paradigm.

There are various definitions and concepts of personality as a system in contemporary personality psychology. One concrete model is the Five-Factor Theory (FFT) Personality System model (McCrae and Costa 2008), an elaboration of the basic Big Five traits approach that defined extraversion, conscientiousness, openness, agreeableness and neuroticism as the basic personality traits of a person. FFT applies a system perspective that connects the Big Five traits with other, more changeable components of an individual's personality, such as characteristic adaptations and self-concept. Figure 2.1 shows this FFT model as applied to the entrepreneurial personality/ mindset (Obschonka and Stuetzer 2017).

According to this model, an entrepreneurial personality or mindset has three major components that interact with each other. They also interact with the social ecology of everyday life and with entrepreneurial outcomes, ranging

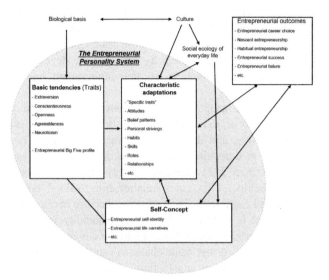

Note: Adapted from the Five-Factor Theory (FFT) Personality System model of McCrae and Costa (2008).
Source: Obschonka and Stuetzer (2017).

Figure 2.1   Psychological characteristics of the individual: a holistic perspective

from entrepreneurial behaviors to entrepreneurial success and failure. These three major components are basic tendencies, characteristic adaptations and self-concept. Basic tendencies stand for the relatively stable basic personality characteristics of a person such as the Big Five traits. They are "broad individual differences in behavior, thought, and feeling that account for general consistencies across situations and over time" (McAdams and Pals 2006, p. 212). They can be seen as one channel through which biology affects entrepreneurship (Nicolaou et al. 2008; Shane et al. 2010). Such basic tendencies are an important component of an entrepreneurial personality or mindset as they represent the basic character of a person which can be understood as the relatively stable core of the personality or a stable reference point in a person's development over the life-span. These basic tendencies shape a person's personality system by affecting the development of characteristic adaptations to the environment and the self-concept.

Characteristic adaptations to the environment are more malleable traits or, to be more precise, "specific motivational, social-cognitive, and developmental variables that are contextualized in time, situations, and social roles" (McAdams and Pals 2006, p. 212). These personality characteristics span attitudes, habits, skills, roles, relationships, values, beliefs, interests and cognitions. They are characteristic because their development is influenced by basic personality tendencies (e.g., how a person *typically* adapts to the environment as an expression of his or her basic character) and they are adaptations because they are substantially shaped by the environment (e.g., the opportunity structure in one's personal learning and personality growth). Relevant entrepreneurial characteristic adaptations are, for example, entrepreneurial self-efficacy, risk-taking, need for achievement, locus of control, and also entrepreneurial attitudes, values, motives and cognitions. These characteristic adaptations "vary tremendously across cultures, families, and portions of the lifespan" (McCrae and Costa 2008, p. 164) because they are so closely linked to the environmental and developmental contexts of a person. One could probably say that they are the most visible components of an entrepreneurial personality or mindset – and indeed many entrepreneurship scholars emphasize their relevance for entrepreneurial outcomes.

Finally, the self-concept represents the person's identity and life narrative, the sense of subjective individuality and self-image. Like the basic tendencies, they might be less visible and easy to articulate than the characteristic adaptation of the personality system. However, the self-concept is another important component of the entrepreneurial personality or mindset (Mmbaga et al. 2020). It guides the development of characteristic adaptions, for instance due to self-verification and self-determination motives (Deci and Ryan 2000). Entrepreneurial passion – which is closely linked to one's identity – is a concrete example of this mechanism (Murnieks et al. 2014; Newman et al. 2021). Moreover, the self-concept gives people a sense of personal purpose, meaning in life and an image of oneself. The environment and learning processes play an important role in the development of the self-concept, for example influenced by the proximal social ecology of everyday life such as parenting and education practices, mass media, job experiences, or the internalization of social roles (Falck et al. 2012). An entrepreneurial self-concept, like entrepreneurial characteristic adaptations, influences entre-preneurial outcomes. Quite often people may choose an entrepreneurial career due to a perceived good fit between entrepreneurship and one's occupational self-concept.

Entrepreneurial outcomes themselves, such as entrepre-neurial activities, success and failure, have the potential to shape the entrepreneurial personality system. This can be regarded as an example of occupational socialization as described by Frese (1982) and others (e.g., Kohn and Schooler 1973). In the logic of this system model, these entrepreneurial outcomes would mainly co-shape characteristic adaptions (e.g., entrepreneurial self-efficacy) and the self-concept (e.g., the development of entrepreneurial identities; see Hoang and Gimeno 2010). However, once more, the basic tendencies in the personality system also shape this adaptation process. In other words, the basic tendencies exert some kind of gravity effect in the development of the entrepreneurial personality system of a person (Obschonka and Stuetzer 2017), or as Roberts et al. (2003) put it: work may make us more of what we already are.

Finally, it is also important to note that a person's person-ality is not static, including the basic tendencies – a myriad of personality research has shown that personality as a system and single isolated personality traits and other components of the personality system do change and develop over time (over the whole life course). The personality psychology literature offers a range of explanation models that go far beyond the simplistic distinction between selection and socialization effects (see, e.g., Roberts 2018; Specht et al. 2014).

A geography of entrepreneurial personality, approached from this personality-oriented paradigm, therefore studies the geographical variation of components of the entrepreneurial personality system (and the geographical variation of the entrepreneurial personality system itself). It tries to understand the macro-psychology of a region or place by applying person-oriented micro-level psychology concepts. In other words, it acknowledges the importance of the *who* question. While it may make sense to question the usefulness of a personality perspective when solely focusing on individual-level entrepreneurial actions and their immediate, situative psychological regulation in context (Frese 2009; Gartner 1988; Ramoglou et al. 2020), entrepreneurship occurs in a wider psychological spatial context that in itself has important and complex effects. The *who* question is not only relevant when studying entrepreneurship at the individual level but also for our understanding of the macro-psychology of regions affecting, and interacting with, entrepreneurship.

Individuals do have a personality – a sense of individuality, stability, identity and life narrative – and this has important implications for entrepreneurship research, practice and policy. Psychological approaches to entrepreneurship should therefore attempt to integrate this psychological reality of people into their concepts and studies. As William James (1890), the father of American psychology, put it: "psychology is the science of mental life". We may thus never *understand* the people side of entrepreneurship if we do not adequately address this mental life (e.g., if we try to narrow it down to psychological factors and mechanisms directly related to concrete actions).

3. Geographic variation of psychological factors associated with entrepreneurship

3.1 PERSONALITY TRAITS AND PROFILES

3.1.1 National differences in McClelland's need for achievement

One particularly influential scholar for scholarly investigation of the geography of entrepreneurial psychology was David McClelland. He was an expert on human motivation as a central component of human productivity. He studied different motives in human motivation (McClelland 1987) and one of his core interests was achievement motivation – the general personal motive to excel and succeed across various projects and contexts. He linked achievement motivation to entrepreneurship (McClelland 1965b) and also to economic development of whole countries (McClelland 1961) – thereby applying a geographical psychological perspective, adopting individual-level psychological concepts and theories to the macro-level (e.g., cultures, societies and the economy as a whole in a given country).

Whereas one can study achievement motivation as trait-like personal characteristics of individuals (e.g., a relatively stable personal motive) with a focus on inter-individual differences

(Judge and Ilies 2002), a particularly interesting aspect of achievement motivation is that it is not just hard-wired but can indeed change over time, as already stressed and shown by McClelland (McClelland 1965a; Miron and McClelland 1979) and later by other motivation researchers, particularly in the fields of human development and educational psychology (Eccles and Wigfield 2002; Heckhausen and Heckhausen 2008; Wigfield et al. 2015). Hence the study of geographical differences in achievement motivation and effects on entrepreneurship and economic development at the societal level can not only deliver insights into macro-psychological drivers of macro-economic outcomes, but also has the potential to inform population-based policy programs aiming to improve economic development by focusing on psychological factors.

McClelland (1961) examined various indicators of achievement motivation in various societies across different historical periods to predict economic development. He also studied historical changes in achievement motivation in a given society and associated subsequent changes in economic performance in the same society, assuming that increases or decreases in collective achievement motivation causally contribute to economic growth and decline, respectively. His book on *The Achieving Society* became a classic read in applied psychology and entrepreneurship research (McClelland 1961).

His ideas on the importance of achievement motivation are still relevant for entrepreneurship research and practice today (Collins et al. 2004; Hisrich et al. 2007; Shane et al. 2003; Stewart and Roth 2007). His pioneering focus on the social ecology and objective geographic aspects relevant for psychological research and its application in society and policymaking are generally regarded as path-breaking in the wider field of geographical psychology (Oishi and Graham 2010). However, the causal (positive) effect of various measures of country-level achievement motivation on economic performance have remained a subject of intense scholarly debate until today (e.g., Beugelsdijk and Smeets 2008; Freeman

1976; Gilleard 1989; Lea et al. 1987; Mazur and Rosa 1977; Schatz 1965; Steel et al. 2018). Part of this discussion is the valid measurement of country differences in achievement motivation, and psychological traits in general. Unlike hard economic indicators, psychological characteristics are more difficult to measure and to compare across cultures and countries. Nonetheless, McClelland's pioneering work on the psychology of entrepreneurship and his interest in geographical aspects of psychological constructs and their relevance for society and the economy as a whole in a given country remains a major milestone in the history of entrepreneurship research and applied psychology. The idea that something as encompassing as a society's economic performance and growth can be linked to an aggregate individual psychological construct to get something done and to be successful in life (cf., Wilson et al. 2014) has proven fascinating and promising, but also controversial (Gurven 2018; Kashima et al. 2019; Schulz et al. 2019).

3.1.2　Big Five traits

Whereas McClelland focused on motivation to understand spatial variation in entrepreneurship, recently there is renewed interest in studying the link between collective mental characteristics and geographical variation in entrepreneurship. This recent research has shifted the focus towards the Big Five model of personality and regional co-variation between these Big Five traits and entrepreneurship. When applying the Five-Factor Theory (FFT) Personality System model (McCrae and Costa 2008), the broad Big Five traits can be interpreted as the basic tendencies in a person's personality system, and McClelland's need for achievement would stand for a certain characteristic adaptation of that individual (influenced by the basic tendencies, but also by developmental and learning contexts, and the individual self-concept) (Obschonka and Stuetzer 2017). In other words, the recent renaissance in empirical geographical research dealing with the psychology of entrepreneurship places an emphasis on the relatively stable dispositions of individuals. Studying the regional variation of personality traits such as the Big Five offers a new perspective on what economists often coin soft regional factors that shape the local economy but which are difficult to conceptualize and to quantify (Audretsch et al. 2019; Florida 2010; Huggins and Thompson 2019). Various economic theories on local entrepreneurial eco-systems and regional differences in entrepreneurial activity increasingly highlight the role of local behavioral and psychological foundations as a crucial determinant of economic outcomes (Fitjar and Rodríguez-Pose 2011; Huggins and Thompson 2019; Saxenian 1996; Sternberg 2009). Various entrepreneurship scholars have emphasized the promise of geographical research looking at *aggregate* psychological traits, aggregated from empirical individual level measures of relatively stable psychological characteristics (Davidsson 1995; Davidsson and Wiklund 1997; Freytag and Thurik 2007).

At least two recent advancements have paved the way for a new generation of studies on the geography of entrepreneurial psychology. First, technological progress has enabled the collection and analysis of psychological big data at the individual level, which can also be used for geographical analyses. For example, internet-based large-scale personality studies provide psychometrically sound personality tests to the wider public and thereby collect personality data from millions of individuals via self-report online questionnaires (e.g., Gosling et al. 2004; Obschonka 2017). Another example is social media methods that translate language used on social media into regional personality traits (e.g., Boyd and Pennebaker 2017; Obschonka et al. 2020a; Pennebaker et al. 2015). Second, theoretical advancements also play an important role, for example in the narrower field of geographical psychology (Rentfrow et al. 2008: Rentfrow and Jokela 2016) or in the wider field of socioecological psychology (Oishi 2014; Oishi

Table 3.1   Big Five traits and entrepreneurship

Big Five trait	Weak expression	Strong expression	Correlation with individual entrepreneurship
Openness	Conservative, cautious	Inventive, curious	r = 0.36
Conscientiousness	Easy going, careless	Efficient, organized	r = 0.45
Extraversion	Solitary, reserved	Outgoing, energetic	r = 0.22
Agreeableness	Challenging, detached	Compassionate, friendly	r = −0.16
Neuroticism	Secure, confident	Sensitive, nervous	r = −0.37

Source: Correlations with individual entrepreneurship are taken from the meta-analysis in Zhao and Seibert (2006).

and Graham 2010). This delivers the conceptual underpinning and intellectual foundation for the study of regional variation in personality traits and effects on economic outcomes.

Before we jump to the topic of geographical variation in the Big Five personality traits, we first need to explain their relationship with entrepreneurship at the individual level. Table 3.1 depicts the descriptions of a person with a weak or strong expression of the trait and its correlation with individual entrepreneurial activity.

High openness to experience is important for entrepreneurship to detect or develop business ideas. High levels of conscientiousness are arguably beneficial to organize and conduct the many tasks necessary to start a business. High extraversion should be a plus when convincing customers to buy a new product or convince lenders to provide money to the business. Low agreeableness might be important in negotiations with suppliers. Low levels of neuroticism can be an advantage to overcome countless hurdles and not to despair when working long hours on a start-up project. Stated differently, there are arguably few entrepreneurs who are not interested in new ideas, are disorganized, have difficulties in talking to people, lack some kind of ruthlessness and become overwhelmed by small problems. Correlations between traits and entrepreneurship at the individual level range from medium to strong (Zhao and Seibert 2006).

Beside the single traits in isolation, it is often useful to consider an entrepreneurial constellation of the Big Five traits described above (Schmitt-Rodermund 2004, 2007). Focusing on personality profiles follows a holistic, person-oriented personality perspective (described in Chapter 2.4) that aims to describe the basic character of a person (Magnusson and Törestad 1993). From this perspective, a basic entrepreneurial character of a person can be studied by means of such a holistic personality perspective that tries to understand the entrepreneurial character of an individual (e.g., in contrast to the isolated effect of single traits, which follows a variable-oriented perspective; see Magnusson and Törestad 1993). Indeed, correlations between an entrepreneurial constellation of the traits and entrepreneurship are larger compared to those of single traits (e.g., Obschonka and Stuetzer 2017).

How can such an entrepreneurial constellation of traits be measured? Consistent with profile similarity research (e.g., with Cronbach and Gleser's *D2*, 1953) and research on prototypical personality profiles (e.g., Asendorpf and van Aken 1999; Block 1971; Chapman and Goldberg 2011), a person's basic entrepreneurial personality structure can be measured by means of an individual's deviation from a statistical reference profile. In this case the reference point is an extreme entrepreneurial profile that statistically defines the outer limits of each single Big Five dimension within an entrepreneurial personality structure. Each individual's deviation from this reference can be assessed to compute an overall goodness-of-fit measure of his or her entrepreneurial personality structure (e.g., the sum of the squared Euclidian difference between the statistical reference profile and the individual empirical Big Five profile (Obschonka et al. 2013)). This is very similar to the least-squares method as a standard approach in regression analysis, which goes back to Carl Friedrich Gauss (see Stigler 1981).

It is important to emphasize that the statistical reference profile (highest possible value in extraversion, conscientiousness and openness; lowest possible value in agreeableness and neuroticism) does not represent a real person or an ideal or perfect entrepreneur, but rather a fixed statistical extreme profile by means of which each individual's entrepreneurial personality structure can be quantified and summarized into a single index, which we will refer to as entrepreneurial personality profile. This definition does not state that *every* entrepreneur has such a profile or that entrepreneurs are only successful if they show this profile. It is well established that entrepreneurs as a population exhibit great heterogeneity in terms of their personality – just like the real-world phenomenon of entrepreneurship shows great heterogeneity in terms of different business activities and types that can be counted under the entrepreneurship umbrella (Davidsson 2016b). However, research studying entrepreneurial activity, motivation, human and social capital, and entrepreneurial development over the life-span shows that this profile is associated with a higher statistical propensity that a person not only has an entrepreneurial personality character and an entrepreneurial mindset, but also engages in entrepreneurial activity (e.g., thinks and acts entrepreneurially). Hence, it is a statistical marker of an entrepreneurial mindset, and may represent the basic tendencies-level in the entrepreneurial personality system (Obschonka and Stuetzer 2017).

Based on the individual-level research described above, a number of recent studies have investigated the geography of the entrepreneurial personality profile and its underlying traits. To this end, the individual entrepreneurial personality profile or the underlying traits of extraversion, conscientiousness, openness, agreeableness and neuroticism are averaged across the respondents of the regions under study (e.g., Audretsch et al. 2017; Fritsch, Obschonka and Wyrwich 2019; Garretsen et al. 2018; Obschonka et al. 2013; Stuetzer et al. 2018). The main intention of these early papers was to test whether there are relationships between the regional aggregated personality characteristics and regional socioeconomic characteristics and whether these relationships resemble the respective individual-level correlations. This is important because one cannot assume that every relationship at the individual level plays out at the aggregate level (Rentfrow et al. 2008; Rentfrow and Jokela 2016). Such an assumption would be like falling prey to the ecological fallacy that needs to be avoided (Robinson 1950).

The first of these path-breaking studies is Rentfrow et al.'s (2008) analysis on regional variation of the Big Five traits in the USA. The authors analyzed self-report personality data from over half a million US residents and found substantial state-level correlations between single Big Five traits and indicators of social behaviors such as crime, social involvement, religiosity and health, even after controlling for socio-demographic factors. For instance, state-level agreeableness was negatively related to state-level indicators of antisocial behavior such as robbery per capita. The authors argue that regional personality differences become expressed and manifested at the geographical level because individual personality affects individual behavior. If certain personalities are more common in a state, this would result in higher rates of particular behaviors on the population level. This expression of regional personality differences should be further amplified by corresponding regional norms and values (partly derived from the regional personality make-up), which influence behavioral tendencies of people in that region, "even if those tendencies are contrary to their natural dispositions" (p. 344).

Obschonka et al. (2013) re-analyzed the personality dataset Rentfrow et al. (2008) had used by first calculating the entrepreneurial personality profile for each study participant (the sum of the squared Euclidian differences between the statistical reference profile and the individual empirical Big Five profile), averaging this profile over the participants of the region and then looking at the regional entrepreneurial personality profile linked to entrepreneurial activity. The regional level of US states was relatively coarse-grained, but the study also looked at a more fine-grained spatial level – major US cities. The authors had hypothesized that the individual-level link between the profile and entrepreneurship would also be present at the regional level. The data indeed revealed that the entrepreneurship-prone personality profile shows regional variation (it shows variance at the regional level), with substantial correlations to entrepreneurial activity (e.g., regional start-up rate) that is also robust when controlling for economic determinants of entrepreneurship across regions.

Figure 3.1 shows the US map for this entrepreneurship-prone personality profile (based on a newer, more recent version of the dataset Rentfrow et al. (2008) used, with more than three million personality tests). At a descriptive level, the spatial patterns in this profile are highly interesting. One can see stronger regional values in the American West and in Florida and lower values in the American Rust Belt and in large parts of the Deep South (e.g., Alabama and Mississippi). Based on Rentfrow et al.'s (2008) theory of the emergence, persistence and manifestation of regional psychological variation, Obschonka et al. (2013) speculated whether selective historical migration patterns as well as cross-generational local socialization through prevalent institutions (e.g., type of industry and work characteristics) might have contributed to this regional differentiation of the psychological map of the USA. This is one example of many of how the geographical study of psychological characteristics can lead to completely new research questions that go beyond the typical study canon in individual-level psychological research.

Figure 3.1 also shows the US map for entrepreneurial activity – how many in the adult population actually start a new business (new businesses per capita). This economic map shows substantial spatial overlap to the psychological map, which is also reflected in substantial region-level bivariate correlations and partial correlations when controlling for

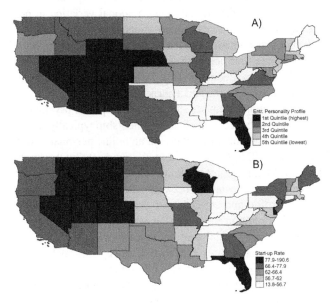

Note: The personality map is based on 2,859,005 personality tests. The measure of entrepreneurship is number of start-ups (every new business establishment with at least one employee) per 1,000 employed in the period from 2003 to 2015.
Source: Updated analysis based on the original in Obschonka et al. (2013).

Figure 3.1   *Regional distribution of an entrepreneurial personality profile and entrepreneurial behavior in the contiguous USA*

other determinants of regional entrepreneurship. Obschonka et al. (2013) replicated this region-level association between the entrepreneurial profile and entrepreneurial activity for major US cities and also in two independent studies looking at regions in Germany and the UK. This provided robust evidence indicating that regional differences in entrepreneurial activity can be more comprehensively explained when considering, and directly studying, regional variation in personality. It thus followed the footprints of the earlier research endeavors that championed and illustrated the promise of the aggregate trait perspective to the study of spatial differences in entrepreneurship (Davidsson 1995; Davidsson and Wiklund 1997; Freytag and Thurik 2007).

While regional analyses studying geographical psychological patterns in the context of entrepreneurship typically rely on self-report questionnaire data (e.g., an online personality test) (Davidsson 1995; Davidsson and Wiklund 1997; Obschonka et al. 2015), a more recent study asked whether one can also replicate the association between the entrepreneurial personality profile and entrepreneurial activity when exploiting another information source for the geography of entrepreneurial psychology – social media (Obschonka et al. 2020a). Do digital footprints from social media convey information that can be used to estimate (in terms of a statistical marker of) the economic dynamics of regions? Can the geography of entrepreneurial psychology be captured from the language used in the Twitter tweets of individuals living in specific locations, instead of relying on millions of questionnaire-based personality tests? Could one use publicly available social media data to estimate soft characteristics of entrepreneurial regions and eco-systems, which are so difficult to assess (Audretsch et al. 2019)?

Psychological research has made great advances in the last decade in the field of estimating personality characteristics from language patterns (Boyd and Pennebaker 2017), and this was particularly enabled by the availability of big data such as language patterns used on social media but also other information from social media such as how people endorse other posts or by analyzing their social networks on social media (Boyd et al. 2020; Kosinski et al. 2013, 2016; Park et al. 2015). This potential of social media to estimate private traits of its users has also become the subject of a wider public debate specifically, around psychological targeting of commercial and political campaigns (Matz et al. 2017) and about data privacy in general (Matz et al. 2020). Documentaries such as "The Social Dilemma", discussing how tech social media companies are able to employ AI-enabled psychological profiling (*The New York Times*, 2020), have further spurred this public debate.

Figure 3.2 illustrates the central result of the social media-based study of the regional variation in the entrepreneurship-prone personality profile in the USA (Obschonka et al. 2020a). The study utilized data from the World Well-Being Project at the University of Pennsylvania (see Park et al. 2015, and http://map.wwbp.org). This project brought together psychologists and data scientists, and derived regional personality estimates (e.g., the single Big Five traits) in a sequence of steps: (a) a machine learning model is used to estimate personality from language use across a sample of 71,556 Facebook users for which language and survey-based self-reported Big Five scores were available; (b) geo-tagging a 10 percent Twitter language sample using data from 5.25 million users; (c) adjusting the Twitter language frequencies appropriately for an application of the Facebook prediction model; and (d) applying the Facebook person-level prediction model to counties on Twitter. This process yielded a final county-level Twitter language sample that included 1.5 billion tweets from the 5.25 million Twitter users for 1,772 counties that represented just under 95 percent of the total US mainland population. These regional Big Five traits were then used to estimate the regional scores in entrepreneurship-prone personality profiles (the entrepreneurial constellation of the Big Five

Note: Entrepreneurial activity was measured with the local start-up rate: # of new firm births per 1,000 people between 2009 and 2015. Dark gray regions in the top figure are hotspots, light gray regions in the top figure are cold spots in the contiguous USA.

Source: Data in A) and B) from Obschonka et al. (2019).

Figure 3.2   *Top A) hotspots and cold spots of an entrepreneurial personality profile (estimated on the basis of 1.5 billion Twitter posts) and bottom B) regional level distribution of entrepreneurial activity in the USA*

traits; Obschonka et al. 2013). This analysis looked at the US county level – a relatively fine-grained spatial level.

The mapping of this Twitter language-based regional entrepreneurial personality profile revealed that large hotspots of entrepreneurial personality (larger areas consistently scoring higher in an entrepreneurial personality) can be found, for example, in the East Coast belt, spanning from Massachusetts all the way to Florida; in Colorado around Denver/Boulder; in San Francisco, the Bay Area and South California; as well as in Gulf Coast regions of Louisiana and Mississippi. Here, particularly entrepreneurially minded people tend to cluster, according to these analyses. In contrast, if one looks at cold spots of *non*-entrepreneurial-minded people, the data revealed that large cold spots are detectable in the Rust Belt, in Southern Texas and in Central California. This descriptive analysis complements the state-level analysis in Obschonka et al. (2013) in that it shows that there can be substantial variation within a given state. For example, California has both hot and cold spots – a pattern one would miss capturing if one looked only at the state level. It is also remarkable that this analysis largely replicated the discovery in Obschonka et al.'s (2013) analysis, that the US Rust Belt is particularly low in entrepreneurial personality features (it is today very non-entrepreneurially minded).

The study then again examined the overlap between the psychological map with the economic map of regional differences in start-up rates. Similar to the earlier results drawing from self-report questionnaire data (e.g., Obschonka et al. 2013), the Twitter-based measure of the entrepreneurial personality profile showed substantial and robust region-level correlations with entrepreneurial activity. In fact, as illustrated in Figure 3.2, the geographic overlap between hot and cold spots of entrepreneurial personality, on the one hand, and the regional level distribution of entrepreneurial activity, on the other, is quite remarkable, indicating that in the powerhouses of entrepreneurial activity the local population that posts on social media uses a particularly "entrepreneurial" language style, reflective of an entrepreneurial personality of these places.

As stressed by Florida (2010), not only individuals but also places (or regions/cities) have a personality as indicated by a growing number of empirical studies on the psychology of regions. The results of this Twitter-based study therefore indicate the usefulness of social media data as a big data source in the study of the geography of entrepreneurial psychology. Social media encodes relevant psychological information that can help explain regional variation in economic activity, in addition to other regional outcomes such as health (Eichstaedt et al. 2015), happiness (Curini et al. 2015) or political orientation (Sylwester and Purver 2015). However, such correlational analyses cannot prove causality (e.g., that a particularly entrepreneurial personality of a place causes high levels of entrepreneurial activity in that place). These analyses first and foremost show that social media language, translated into local personality characteristics, can be a meaningful and robust *statistical marker* of economic activity, which has already important implications not only for research interested in the soft local factors but also for practice and policymaking (e.g., public policy interested in psychological correlates of local entrepreneurial eco-systems; Acs et al. 2017; Sternberg 2009).

Although there is growing evidence from various countries, types of data and geographic levels that the geographical patterns of entrepreneurial psychological characteristics correlate with geographical patterns in entrepreneurial activity, this does not answer the questions of what kind of mechanisms could drive this statistical relationship and whether this link is indeed causal. Regional personality might affect regional economic outcomes but the reverse influence of economic structures on personality characteristics is not unlikely. The link between regional personality and economic outcomes could also simply be spurious in nature – driven by a third variable. In a sense, this is a very similar question to the discussion in the individual-level research on whether personality is indeed a causal shaper of life outcomes, including occupational choice via selection (Schneider et al. 1995), or whether life outcomes such as work characteristics and job performance may shape personality traits via socialization (Frese 1982; Kohn and Schooler 1973; Roberts et al. 2003). The interested reader is also advised to examine Specht et al. (2014) for an overview of other concepts of personality change and development.

From a theoretical perspective, economists have long been arguing that local soft characteristics such as culture or macro-psychological features of places (collective mental characteristics) may indeed causally drive entrepreneurship and regional growth (e.g., Saxenain 1996; see also Beugelsdijk and Maseland 2011; Greif 2006; Guiso et al. 2006). Likewise, various psychologists have also stressed a potentially causal effect of the geography of psychology on economic outcomes (e.g., McClelland 1961; McCrae 2001; Rentfrow et al. 2008).

One way how regional personality differences could shape economic outcomes is via a systematic region-level interaction with local knowledge resources. In a study that puts this assumption to the empirical test by examining this local interaction at the US MSA level (Metropolitan Statistical Areas – larger population centers in the USA) and a similar spatial level in the UK, Obschonka et al. (2015) examined a larger version of the self-report personality questionnaire-based dataset used in Obschonka et al. (2013). The basic idea in this study was to address the *knowledge paradox* in economics, namely the empirical observation that despite the primacy of new knowledge and ideas as the competitive advantage in the modern innovation-driven economy, investments in knowledge resources (e.g., R&D, human capital) alone did not generate more entrepreneurship and economic growth. Something was missing and one candidate were soft factors that many economists deem highly influential but that are difficult to measure. Knowledge resources as such might not lead to more entrepreneurship and economic growth – it might also require a certain level of entrepreneurial psychology (e.g., entrepreneurial mindsets, collective norms, attitudes and personal agency) in a region that such knowledge resources turn into tangible outcomes, perhaps more start-ups and a more vibrant and competitive local economy.

Using the local level in human capital and industry diversity as indicators of knowledge resources, the study (Obschonka et al. 2015) indeed found robust indication that it is particularly the interaction between a higher local level in entrepreneurial personality (the entrepreneurship-prone Big Five profile; Obschonka et al. 2013; Schmitt-Rodermund 2004, 2007) and such knowledge resources that is associated with stronger entrepreneurial activity. This result for the US regions was replicated in the UK. Figures 3.3 and 3.4 show the consistent descriptive overlap of the interaction between entrepreneurial personality and knowledge resources in both countries (USA and UK, respectively) at small spatial levels. Figure 3.5 depicts the nature of the statistical interaction effect in a region-level regression analysis. This clearly shows that when both come together – new knowledge in the region *and* a stronger entrepreneurial psychology in that region in terms of entrepreneurial basic personality tendencies – then the region is likely to be among the top performing places in terms of entrepreneurship. Indeed, these results revealed that the wealthiest region in the USA, San Jose – home of Silicon Valley – not only exhibits relatively high entrepreneurship rates but also high levels in both entrepreneurial personality and knowledge (human capital, industry diversity). The results remained remarkably robust in a number of conservative robustness checks that considered, for example, migration patterns, representativeness issues of the regional personality data regarding age and gender, and alternative explanations of the findings (e.g., whether the region's employment share in creative occupations confounds these results; see Florida 2004).

The authors also found this interaction when focusing solely on high-impact firms – firms with exceptional growth, taken from the 100 fastest-growing US firms as listed by *Fortune* magazine (Fortune 100) and a comparable list of 100 firms with the fastest growth published by the *Sunday Times* and Virgin for Great Britain (Fast Track 100). The results showed that more than 75 percent of US-based Fortune 100 firms and 66 percent of UK-based Fast Track 100 firms are located in regions with above-median levels for *both* of the measures of entrepreneurial personality and knowledge (or, in more colloquial terms, where new knowledge meets an entrepreneurially minded population). In contrast, less than 5 percent of Fortune 100 and less than 15 percent of Fast Track 100 firms are from regions with below median levels for *both* the measures of knowledge and entrepreneurial personality. These additional analyses of firms with exceptional growth underscore the statistical robustness of the knowledge–culture interaction effect when considering such an alternative measure of entrepreneurship.

While these mechanism-focused analyses that look at potential processes of how regional personality differences might shape the local economy, such as Obschonka et al.'s (2015) study, cannot prove causality, they at least suggest that one potential secret of local economic prosperity in today's innovation-driven economies is a local interaction between entrepreneurial psychology and the production of new knowledge. This, in a way, is very consistent with seminal theorizing in regional economics on the hard to measure local mechanisms that drive competitive advantage of regions (Audretsch et al. 2019; Saxenain 1996; see also Huggins and Thompson 2019). Hence, these empirical results are a prime example of how the geography of entrepreneurial psychology not only informs knowledge in geographical psychology but also advances knowledge in economics and human geography.

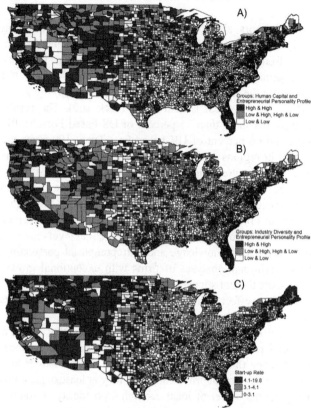

Note: A) interaction human capital and entrepreneurial personality
profile; B) interaction industry diversity and entrepreneurial personality
profile; and C) average start-up rate 2004–11. Industry diversity is
computed as the inverse of the Herfindahl index of industry employment.
The start-up rates are computed as the number of business births per 1,000
employees. B) should be interpreted as follows: both variables, industry
diversity and the entrepreneurial personality profile, were split at the
median. Unshaded regions have below median values in industry diversity
and the entrepreneurial personality profile. Regions in light gray are above
median in either industry diversity or the entrepreneurial personality profile.
Regions in dark gray have above median values in industry diversity and
the entrepreneurial personality profile. C) can be interpreted in the same

way while interaction groups are created regarding high human capital (Bachelor degree or above) and the entrepreneurial personality profile. *Source:*   Updated analysis based on Obschonka et al. (2015). The personality data are taken from the Gosling–Potter Personality Project (http://personality-project.org/). Data on human capital are taken from the American Community Survey (ACS) (2006–10) (https://www.census .gov/programs-surveys/acs). Data on industry diversity stem from the ACS (2006–11). Data on start-ups are taken from Statistics of U.S. Businesses (SUSB) (https://www.census.gov/programs-surveys/susb.html).

Figure 3.3   Interaction between knowledge resources (human capital and industry diversity) and an entrepreneurial personality profile across US counties

They illustrate the real-world importance of the geography of entrepreneurial psychology, and also the effectiveness of interdisciplinary work and research teams that combine expertise in psychology with expertise in economics and human geography (Obschonka 2019).

Another promising study context in which the geography of entrepreneurial psychology can deliver important insights is the study of crises and how regions and local populations react to them. Studying crises through an entrepreneurship lens has become an important research topic in the social sciences (Doern 2016; Shepherd and Williams 2014, 2018; Williams and Vorley 2014). Such crises can range from major macro-economic crises and shocks, and other global crises (e.g., health crisis like the COVID-19 pandemic or refugee crises) to more localized major disruptions of society such as natural disasters or war.

Obschonka et al. (2016) examined the impact of the 2007/08 global financial crisis (GFC), which put the global economy into a major recession and was the worst economic collapse since the Great Depression of the late 1920s and 1930s (Hausman and Johnston 2014). Such major economic crises pose substantial threats to the prosperity of regions by triggering a massive, instant slowdown of local economies

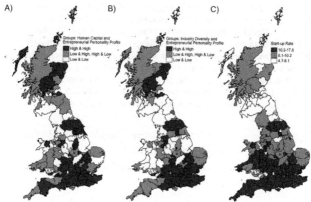

Note: A) interaction human capital and entrepreneurial personality
profile; B) interaction industry diversity and entrepreneurial personality
profile; and C) average start-up rate 2004–11. Industry diversity is
computed as the inverse of Herfindahl index of industry employment. The
start-up rates are computed as the number of business births per 1,000
employees. B) should be interpreted as follows: both variables, industry
diversity and the entrepreneurial personality profile, were split at the
median. Unshaded regions have below median values in industry diversity
and the entrepreneurial personality profile. Regions in light gray are above
median in either industry diversity or the entrepreneurial personality profile.
Regions in dark gray have above median values in industry diversity and
the entrepreneurial personality profile. C) can be interpreted in the same
way while interaction groups are created regarding high human capital
(level-4 qualification or above) and the entrepreneurial personality profile.
Source: Updated analysis based on Obschonka et al. (2015). The
personality data are taken from the BBC Lab Project (no longer available).
Data on human capital are taken from the Office for National Statistics
(ONS) (https://www.ons.gov.uk/). Data on industry diversity stem from
the 2011 Census (https://www.ons.gov.uk/census/2011census). Data on
start-ups are taken from the Inter-Departmental Business Register (IDBR)
(https://www.ons.gov.uk/aboutus/whatwedo/paidservices/interdepartmental
businessregisteridbr).

Figure 3.4   *Interaction between knowledge resources
(human capital and industry diversity)
and an entrepreneurial personality profile
across British counties*

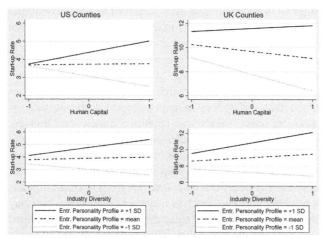

Note: (Top) interaction between human capital and entrepreneurial personality profile; (bottom) interaction between industry diversity and entrepreneurial personality profile.
Source: Updated analysis based on Obschonka et al. (2015).

Figure 3.5   Interaction plots between knowledge resources (human capital and industry diversity) and an entrepreneurial personality profile in US counties (left) and British counties (right)

(Stiglitz 2010), with potential long-term consequences for the economic trajectories of regions and the prosperity of the people living in them (Elder 1999). Scholars and policy-makers are thus highly interested in a better understanding of regional factors contributing to economic resilience of regions and populations – what are the protective factors that help regions endure crises in a less vulnerable way (Martin 2012; Martin and Sunley 2015)?

For the study of protective effects of regional psychological characteristics, the GFC can be seen as a particularly suitable study context since it was, in its severity and scope, largely unforeseeable and even surprised leading economists (Krugman 2009). Standard macro-economic models (often based on rational decision-making) struggled to explain the crisis but also why some regions fared better during the crisis than others (indicative of local economic resilience). Seminal psychological research at the individual level has shown that differences in psychological features, such as emotions, traits, values and cognitive biases, can augment purely rational models of micro-economic behavior (Tversky and Kahneman 1974). Hence, similar psychological factors at the regional level might help shed light on the "irrational" economically beneficial reactions of regions to crisis. Regions as a whole will thus react to major crises in ways that may appear "irrational" in the sense that they cannot be explained by a mechanistic view that focuses solely on the region's economic infrastructure and rational decision-making. Rather, macro-psychological features are likely to play a significant role. Obschonka et al. (2016) therefore examined whether the macro-psychological factor of a regional entrepreneurial personality profile adds significant explanatory value to existing models predicting regional economic resilience. They also examined the extent to which the findings are replicated within the USA and the UK – two major economies that were hit massively by the crisis.

Explaining the change in the local start-up rate during the GFC, as an indicator of the extent of the local economic slowdown during a major crisis, the study showed that those regions scoring higher in the entrepreneurial personality profile (Obschonka et al. 2013; Schmitt-Rodermund 2004, 2007) showed a substantially weaker or even no decline in the local start-up rate during the crisis than other regions in the same country. This effect, which also holds when looking at regional levels in neuroticism alone, was replicated in both countries under study. Figures 3.6 and 3.7 illustrate these protective effects. Interestingly, with regard to causality, it is unlikely that selection migration before and during the crisis could have driven these results in a way not where regional personality shapes economic resilience but more where entrepreneurial and emotionally stable people moved into the economically resilient regions before and during the crisis. As mentioned above, the crisis was largely unforeseeable (Krugman 2009). Although this study could also not test for strict causality, it seems plausible to assume that regional personality differences indeed contributed in a causal manner to local economic resilience.

Obschonka et al.'s (2016) study was among the first to present major empirical evidence for the protective effect offered by macro-psychological features against an economic slowdown during a major economic crisis. The results thus suggest that the assets and liabilities of a region shaping its economic performance and prosperity are not limited to characteristics of the economic infrastructure but also include the underlying psychology of the region (Beugelsdijk and Maseland 2011; Greif 2006; Guiso et al. 2006; McClelland 1961). Recent research endeavors have broadened the scope in crisis research considering geographical psychology by not only looking at macro-economic crises (e.g., Garretsen et al. 2020) but also examining various other types of crisis (e.g., health; see Peters et al. 2020).

If the geography of entrepreneurial psychology can help to explain regional differences in entrepreneurial activity and economic resilience, can it also contribute to a deeper understanding of regional growth? This fundamentally important question was addressed in the study by Stuetzer et al. (2018), again based on the self-report questionnaire-based personality data that was utilized in the earlier studies (Obschonka et al. 2013, 2015, 2016). At the level of Metropolitan Statistical Areas (MSAs), the authors found a clear connection between the regional entrepreneurial personality profile and employment growth. As depicted in Figure 3.8, MSAs with a more entrepreneurially minded populace enjoyed more economic

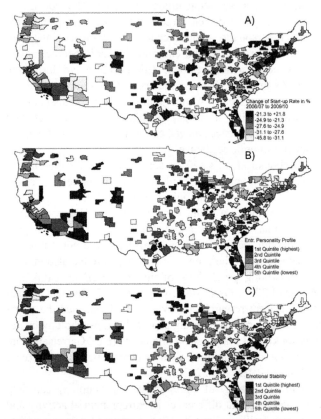

Note: A) change in start-up rate between 2006/07 and 2009/10; B) entrepreneurial personality profile; and C) emotional stability. The start-up rates are computed as the number of business births per 1,000 employees. The change in the start-up rates are computed as the change between the average of the 2006 and 2007 start-up rates, and the average of the 2009 and 2010 start-up rates as a percentage.
Source: Data on start-ups are taken from the SUSB (https://www.census .gov/programs-surveys/susb.html). The personality data are taken from the Gosling–Potter Personality Project (http://personality-project.org/). Updated analysis based on Obschonka et al. (2016).

Figure 3.6   Personality and entrepreneurship in the global financial crisis in US cities

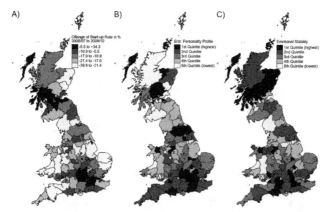

Note: A) change in start-up rate between 2006/07 and 2009/10; B) entrepreneurial personality profile; C) emotional stability. The start-up rates are computed as the number of business births per 1,000 employees. The change in the start-up rates are computed as the change between the average of the 2006 and 2007 start-up rates, and the average of the 2009 and 2010 start-up rates as a percentage.
Source: Data on start-ups are taken from the IDBR (https://www.ons.gov .uk/aboutus/whatwedo/paidservices/interdepartmentalbusinessregisteridbr). The personality data are taken from the BBC Lab Project. Updated analysis based on Obschonka et al. (2016).

Figure 3.7   *Personality and entrepreneurship in the global financial crisis in British counties*

growth between 2000 and 2015. This result was replicated by a different study investigating economic growth in UK cities (Garretsen et al. 2020).

This finding naturally raises two questions: (1) What are the mechanisms behind this correlation; and (2) is it causal? Regarding mechanisms, an entrepreneurially minded population in a region is more likely to start new businesses, which in turn accelerates growth (Fritsch and Wyrwich 2019). Beside starting own companies, entrepreneurially minded employees can also be a key driver for innovative activities in existing firms, allowing them to grow through the development of

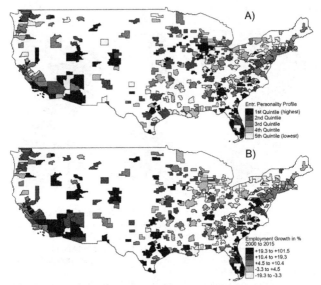

Note: A) entrepreneurial personality profile; and B) employment growth. Employment growth is computed as the change between the 2015 employment level and the 2000 employment level as a percentage.
Source: The personality data are taken from the Gosling–Potter Personality Project (http://personality-project.org/). Employment data are taken from the U.S. Bureau of Labor Statistics (https://www.bls.gov/news .release/empsit.toc.htm). Updated analysis based on Stuetzer et al. (2018).

Figure 3.8   *Entrepreneurial personality profile and economic growth in US cities*

new technologies and products (Caragliu, Del Bo et al. 2016). Regarding causality, it is possible that the above described mechanisms work in the opposite direction too: entrepreneurially minded people might migrate to growing regions with more start-ups and innovative firms in order to capitalize on available economic opportunities but also to find a better match between their individual personality and the personalities at their workplace and neighborhood. There are numerous stories of prospective entrepreneurs moving to Silicon Valley for both reasons (Saxenian 1999). In short, there are good arguments for a reciprocal relationship between entrepreneurially minded people and economic growth.

Stuetzer et al. (2018) tackle the question of causality with a method known as instrumental variable regression. Although widely used in economics, it is relatively new in psychology. For this reason, we will devote some text explaining this method. The lay reader familiar with this method may want to skip this paragraph. The main idea of the approach in Stuetzer et al. (2018) and Glaeser et al. (2015) is to use an exogenous variation in the presence of entrepreneurially minded people. Much of the industrialization in Europe and the USA was driven by the availability of coal as an energy source in the eighteenth and nineteenth centuries. Regions with or near coal deposits enjoyed low coal prices, which led to location and growth of specific industries such as metal manufacturing and textile. These were large-scale industries, employing thousands of workers with a pronounced division of labor. Scholars argue that in such firms entrepreneurial skills and mindsets do not flourish, leaving regions dominated by these industries with a shortage of potential entrepreneurs (Glaeser et al. 2015). This exogenous variation in entrepreneurially minded people enables a two-stage regression approach. In the first stage, the regional entrepreneurial personality profile is explained by the presence of coalfields. From this regression a predicted entrepreneurial personality profile is computed that reflects only the regional variation of the coal deposits. This predicted entrepreneurial personality profile is then used to explain variation in economic growth. By doing so, only the coal-related variation in the regional presence of entrepreneurially minded people is used to explain variation in economic growth. As there is no backward effect of economic growth on the location of the coalfields, the endogeneity problem is circumvented and one is able to estimate a causal effect of the presence of entrepreneurially minded people on economic growth.

3.1.3   Other traits

Beside the Big Five model, empirical projects on the geography of entrepreneurial psychology have also started to look at other personality characteristics and their regional distribution and co-variation with entrepreneurship. For example, Ebert et al. (2019b) introduced a new large-scale psychological dataset of almost 400,000 US residents and focused on regional differences in courage (Rate 2010). Courage can be interpreted as a characteristic adaption in the entrepreneurial personality system, in the language of the Five-Factor Theory (FFT) personality system model (McCrae and Costa 2008; Obschonka and Stuetzer 2017). At the individual level, courage is often seen as an important psychological feature of entrepreneurs, as the "*sine qua non* virtue for entrepreneurs" (Naughton and Cornwall 2006, p. 73), but empirical studies examining courage as a characteristic of the entrepreneurial mindset are still very scarce.

Ebert et al. (2019b) utilized data collected in the *Time Magazine* Ultimate Harry Potter Fan Quiz project that employed a self-report personality questionnaire (including items measuring courage) as the basis for sorting each respondent into a Hogwarts House as defined in the Harry Potter novels (see https://time.com/4809884/harry-potter-house -sorting-hat-quiz/). Hence, by means of such highly popular fictional literature it was possible to collect personality data from the wider general public (assuming that Harry Potter fans are not substantially overrepresented in a certain social group). As in the Gosling–Potter Personality Project (Gosling et al. 2004; Rentfrow et al. 2008), the questionnaire also included sociodemographic items that allowed respondents to be assigned to regions (e.g., items asking for the respondent's zip code). The mapping of courage showed a systematic pattern (Figure 3.9), again consistent with the notion that psychological characteristics can show geographical system-atical variation (Rentfrow et al. 2008; Rentfrow and Jokela 2016). Hotspots of courage were identified in an extensive area reaching from California, Arizona, Utah, Colorado and

Note: Courage was measured with a seven-item scale. Data stem from an internet survey of 390,431 respondents between 2017 and 2018. Dark gray regions are hotspots, light gray regions are cold spots in contiguous US MSAs.
Source: Updated analysis based on Ebert et al. (2020).

Figure 3.9   *Regional distribution of courage across US MSAs*

New Mexico, to Texas and Oklahoma. Furthermore, the state of Florida also consistently shows increased levels of courage. Cold spots of courage, in turn, were found in an extensive area spanning eastwards from the Midwest (Dakotas, Minnesota, Iowa, Nebraska, Missouri), across the so-called Rust Belt (Illinois, Indiana, Michigan, Pennsylvania, New York, New Jersey) up to Boston and down to the Carolinas.

The results further showed that regional courage, at the US MSA level, positively predicts entrepreneurship – more courageous populations also have higher start-up rates. This effect held when controlling for regional human capital and knowledge assets, regional economic structure, regional prosperity, business size distribution across regional start-up cohorts (to account for an elevated number of regional start-ups due to many small-scale entrepreneurial projects) and urbanity (population density). The authors not only looked at entrepreneurial activity, but also at entrepreneurial survival/ failure (share of start-ups that were still in operation five years after their foundation), an important topic in contemporary entrepreneurship research (Brüderl et al. 1992; Shepherd 2003). Research in economic geography often indicates that regional factors fostering the emergence of new firms often negatively relate to their survival after foundation (Brixy and Grotz 2007). The data analyzed in Ebert et al. (2020) indicated that regional courage is indeed not positively but negatively associated with entrepreneurial survival (in regions with more courageous populations the average start-up survived for a shorter time across the first five years of operation than the average start-up in other regions). How can this be explained?

Regional courage might not only make adventurous behavioral tendencies more likely, but also an underestimation of risks. The data indeed showed that regional differences in economic risk-taking is a valid mediator between regional courage and entrepreneurial survival. Hence, stronger local courage could foster a riskier approach to entrepreneurship in the region – which could be a double-edged sword. This risky, enterprising behavior can have benefits (e.g., more start-ups and a general economic vitality) but potentially also unproductive consequences (e.g., more entrepreneurial failure) with economic and psychosocial costs for entrepreneurs and regions (Brüderl et al. 1992; Coad 2014; Shepherd 2003).

This type of research illustrates the promise of geographical studies into the psychology of entrepreneurship not only for the scholarly investigation of entrepreneurial activity at the spatial level, but also for the study of geographical patterns of entrepreneurial success and failure.

3.2 CREATIVE CLASS APPROACH

Another important approach to conceptualize and study relevant "soft" factors of places and regions in the modern economy is focusing on the creativity of places and regions. Creativity as a source of growth has gained increasing attention in recent years. It is defined as the ability to generate new knowledge or to recombine existing knowledge in new ways, thereby generating new ideas or products (Amabile et al. 2005; Runco 2004; Sternberg and Lubart 1996). Creativity is an ability inherent in all people who find ways to express their creativity in many different fields. Creativity can have many forms: artistic, technological and economic. Particularly relevant for entrepreneurship are the setting up of a new firm or organization and the transformation of knowledge into marketable products, i.e., innovation. Both types of creativity can be important drivers of regional growth.

Key research questions on creativity are "Who are the creative people?", "What makes people creative?" and "What determines the distribution of creative people in space?" In his influential book *The Rise of the Creative Class* (2004), Richard Florida empirically identified creative people by their occupation. Florida's creative class consists of people that "engage in complex problem solving that involves a great deal of independent judgment and requires high levels of education of human capital. ... Those [...] in the Creative Class are primarily paid to create and have considerable more autonomy and flexibility than the other [...] classes to do so" (p. 8). According to Florida, the core of the creative class includes "people in science and engineering, architecture and design, education, arts, music and entertainment, whose economic function is to create new ideas, new technology and/or new creative content" (p. 8). Surrounding this creative core is "a broader group of creative professionals in business and finance, law, health care and related fields". An important subgroup of the creative core is the bohemians, which includes artistically creative people such as "authors, designers, musicians, composers, actors, directors, painters, sculptors, artists, printmakers, photographers, dancers, artists, and performers" (p. 333).[1]

Florida argues that artistic, technological and cultural creativity are deeply interrelated: "Not only do they share a common thought process, they reinforce each other through cross-fertilization and mutual stimulation" (2004, p. 33). This could mean geographic coincidence of the different dimensions of creativity or coincidence at the level of individuals.[2] Florida particularly argues that people with high ambitions of becoming self-employed prefer locations which are characterized by high levels of cultural creativity. However, the geographic coincidence of cultural creativity and entrepreneurship does not necessarily suggest a coincidence at the level of individuals. The reason for geographic coincidence may simply be that the regional levels of new business formation and of cultural activity depend on the same factors, while entrepreneurs and creative people are different persons. Lee et al. (2004) attempt to investigate such relationships for the USA by asking if regions with a high level of cultural

---

[1]   An important critique of Florida's classification of "creative" occupations is that most of these occupations require a relatively high level of qualification, so that his approach may mainly indicate qualification, not creativity (Glaeser 2005). Empirical studies indeed show a close statistical relationship between the regional shares of highly educated population (e.g., those with a tertiary degree) and of those working in creative class occupations. As a result of this close correlation, attempts to distinguish the contribution of the two factors to regional growth led to rather mixed results (Boschma and Fritsch 2009; McGranahan and Wojan 2007; Florida et al. 2008).

[2]   For an analysis of coincidence at the micro-level of individuals, see Fritsch and Sorgner (2014).

activity are also characterized by a correspondingly high level of start-ups. Indeed, they find some coincidence of these two types of creativity at a regional level and conclude that there may be a close relationship.

Florida (2004) suggests that creative people do not solely base their decision to live in a certain location because of job opportunities available there. For Florida, factors such as the variety of the cultural supply, tolerance and openness towards new ideas, towards people of different ethnic background, of different sexual orientation or different styles of living are just as important as the regional labor market to creative individuals. According to Florida, these factors are important for two reasons. First, it is easier for people to integrate in such an environment without having to abandon their own identity. Second, tolerance and openness may lead to variety and diversity. This gives creative people the opportunity to gain new experiences that can be a stimulus and inspiration for the creative process (Andersen and Lorenzen 2005; Florida 2004).

Furthermore, Florida (2004) assumes that creative people prefer a diversity of small-scale cultural activities with a vibrant nightlife and an innovative music scene over traditional cultural events such as museums, operas, ballets or professional sports teams. His recommendation for regional policymakers is, therefore, to create a suitable environment for creative people in order to account for the key importance of this part of the regional population, an argument inspired by Jane Jacobs' (1961, 1969) seminal thinking about the planning of creative urban places (Hospers and van Dalm 2005).

In addition, Florida (2004) applies a number of indicators for openness, tolerance and cultural variety, such as the share of foreign-born population (Melting Pot Index), the share of people in artistic occupations (Bohemian Index) or the share of homosexual people (Gay Index). For the USA and some European countries, two studies provide some evidence for these hypotheses. Boschma and Fritsch (2009) find that in many European countries, bohemians tend to live in regions characterized by a high share of immigrants and cultural activities. Asheim and Hansen (2009) also report positive correlations between the presence of artists and the regional share of creative people in Sweden. The attractive force of bohemia and cultural amenities becomes evident when looking at variables other than population shares. Analyzing a large-scale database of US citizens, Florida, Mellander and Stolarick found that the existence of cultural opportunities is an important determinant of higher community satisfaction. The presence of bohemians is also related to higher housing prices – even when controlling for economic factors (Florida et al. 2008). Some other studies have found that the gay and lesbian population, indicating an open and tolerant climate, is correlated with the presence of the creative class (e.g., Florida et al. 2008; McGranahan and Wojan 2007).

However, correlations and regressions relating the share of people in creative occupation today to the current wealth level or to economic growth are not really convincing because of the ever present chicken and egg problem with regard to the underlying causality: Does the presence of creative people cause growth or do growth and wealth induce spending on cultural amenities? In the latter case, a high share of people in cultural occupations would not be a cause but more a symptom of economic prosperity. Falck, Fritsch and Heblich (2011) tried to overcome this problem by using the presence of an opera house built in the baroque era in Germany before the year 1800 as an indicator for cultural activity. They demonstrate that in the case of Germany, proximity to a baroque opera house still has a significantly positive impact on the regional distribution of high-skilled employees as well as on regional growth today.

Taken together, Florida's radical approach of highlighting creativity of people and places as a key factor of successful regional economies can be considered an important contribution to concepts of those macro-psychological factors of regions and places that are conducive for entrepreneurship.

Although his ideas were not entirely new and based on Jane Jacobs' groundbreaking work (Hospers and van Dalm 2005), they stimulated a new generation of research focusing on soft factors of regions and places (e.g., creative mindsets). One could interpret his approach of measuring creativity of people and places as rather indirect though – his measure of the creative class did not directly assess the creativity of people (e.g., their creative personality) but inferred it indirectly (e.g., by studying creative occupations). The geography of entrepreneurial psychology can deliver new means of measuring creativity of places and regions more directly – by focusing on people's creative personality as a psychological construct for example (Selby et al. 2005).

3.3 CULTURE AND ENTREPRENEURSHIP

When talking about the differences in psychological characteristics of geographical units, we also need to discuss the related concept of entrepreneurship culture. As it is still somewhat unclear what constitutes an (entrepreneurship) culture, its disciplinary roots, definitions and measurement approaches will be discussed, as well as the similarities and differences to psychological characteristics.

3.3.1 Culture

Several disciplines such as economics, psychology, anthropology, management and sociology are interested in the concept of culture. While its disciplinary definitions differ, there is a common core of a human collective influencing individual values, attitudes and beliefs. Among the competing definitions, Hofstede's (2001) view of culture as a "collective programming of the mind, that distinguishes one group from another" (p. 9) stands out in terms of impact and acceptance. This collective programming often takes place at an early age in childhood and adolescence, but also adults can partly socialize into a new culture after migration. The human collective sharing a culture can be teams, organizations or regional and national populations.

Of special interest to us are the approaches to culture in psychology and economics. In psychology the subfield of cross-cultural psychology is interested in mental processes and subsequent human behavior in diverse cultural conditions. This includes very opposite research streams such as cross-cultural differences but also the psychological universals across people from different cultures. The effect of the cultural context on individual developmental processes is also a core topic (Berry et al. 1992; Kashima 2016; Keller and Greenfield 2000; Lehman et al. 2004; Markus and Kitayama 1991). Different from many top-down approaches of culture as context that influences individuals, cross-cultural psychology has also an interest in the construction of culture as a bottom-up process through human interactions (Segall et al. 1998).

In economics, culture has drawn research interest because of its influence on individual information processing and decision-making. As culture is deeply rooted in history, the manifested norms, values and beliefs of a human group provides information to its members on how to behave, what is accepted, what is not and what the consequences of divergent behavior will be (Nunn 2012). In that sense, culture is often regarded as an informal institution – the unwritten rules of the social game (North 1994). Economics is interested in the effects of culture on economic outcomes (e.g., Becker et al. 2011; Cantoni and Yuchtman 2014; Dittmar 2011; Greif 1994) but also on the historical roots of culture (e.g., Alesina et al. 2011; Nunn and Wantchekon 2011; Voigtländer and Voth 2012). The interplay and co-evolution of culture and formal institutions such as the written law is also of interest to economists (Nunn 2012).

Economic and psychological approaches to culture have several things in common. Both acknowledge a dominant top-down effect of shared values, beliefs and norms on a person that has normative force across the individual's development. They also share a focus on the mental processes of information processing and decision-making. It is also acknowledged that culture belongs to the level of social structure that is deeply embedded in a population and that tends to change very slowly over long periods of time. Thus culture can survive considerable shocks to the socioeconomic environment, such as serious economic crises, devastating wars and drastic changes of political regimes (North 1994; Williamson 2000).

3.3.2   Entrepreneurship culture

If we rely on Hofstede's (2001) view on culture, an entrepreneurship culture can be understood as the collective programming of the mind toward entrepreneurial values and beliefs that favors individualism, independence, self-efficacy and motivation for achievement (Beugelsdijk 2007; Stuetzer et al. 2018). A competing conceptualization of entrepreneurial culture is to characterize it as an "aggregate psychological trait" (Freytag and Thurik 2007, p. 123) in the regional population. Thereby, the aggregation is either based on the above described values which are conceptually part of the characteristic adaptations (e.g., Davidsson and Wiklund 1997) described in Chapter 2, or based on the underlying personality traits such as the Big Five. For example, even the authors of this book have used aggregate personality traits as a proxy for entrepreneurship culture (e.g., Fritsch, Obschonka and Wyrwich 2019; Stuetzer et al. 2016).

With this diversity in definitions and thereupon following measurement approaches, the question arises whether the concept of entrepreneurship culture is so broad and fuzzy that nearly everything can be put under this label. We argue that the distinction between the collective programming of the mind and the aggregate trait approach is not sharp. Instead, both concepts are interrelated. Personality traits and characteristic adaptations are arguably key building blocks of individual mental models and influence how individuals process information and make decisions (Denzau and North 1994). Through repeated interactions of individuals, shared mental models of groups can emerge. These shared mental models also influence the information processing of the group members and provide guidance as to what is and what is not accepted behavior. Through its influence on information processing and action, a shared mental model can have a normative influence on people's personality characteristics. Thus, we argue that entrepreneurial culture is neither purely an aggregate personality trait nor purely shared norms and belief systems of groups. In a dynamic setting of change and evolution, an entrepreneurial culture arguably encompasses both approaches.

One important aspect of entrepreneurial culture is the social legitimacy of entrepreneurs and their activities (Etzioni 1987; Kibler et al. 2014; Kibler and Kautonen 2016). As a consequence, the more society views entrepreneurship as a legitimate activity, the higher its demand and the more resources are dedicated to such activity. Furthermore, the acceptance of not only start-up activity but also of failure may be an important element of an entrepreneurship culture. If there is a low stigma attached to failure in a region, this may encourage people to give entrepreneurship a try because the psychological costs of failure are lower than elsewhere (e.g., Wyrwich et al. 2016; Wyrwich et al. 2019). In short, there are many aspects of the regional environment that may be, to different degrees, conducive to new business formation (Dubini 1989).

There is also considerable overlap between the notion of an entrepreneurship culture and the concept of social capital, as has been put forward by Coleman (1988), Putnam (2000) and others (e.g., Fritsch and Wyrwich 2016a). In essence, social capital refers to the social acceptance of certain values and of respective behaviors, trust and particularly the networks of social relationships between actors both public and private (for an overview, see Westlund and Bolton 2003). It includes information channels such as role models that can have a considerable effect on individual behavior. The existence of social capital may not only have a stimulating effect on the decision to start an own business, but it may also be conducive to the quality of the new businesses and their performance. As far as social capital is related to entrepreneurship, the idea goes beyond the concept of an entrepreneurial culture because it includes a system of relationships. The concept of an entrepreneurship culture goes beyond the notion of social capital as it may include supportive institutional and physical infrastructure, or policy layers (Fritsch and Wyrwich 2016a). At the regional level, a context of people with entrepreneurial traits, enterprising individuals, social legitimacy of entrepreneurship, supporting social networks and institutions has been termed entrepreneurship capital (Audretsch and Keilbach 2004) or an entrepreneurial eco-system (Stam 2015).

3.3.3 Measuring entrepreneurship culture

As discussed in the previous section, there are varying definitions of entrepreneurship with differing measurement approaches to suit. We can loosely divide academic empirical papers into studies at the national level and regional level. At the national level, studies dominate that are based on Hofstede's collective programming of the mind approach. Hofstede empirically extracted cultural dimensions of power distance, individualism vs. collectivism, masculinity vs. femininity, and uncertainty avoidance from a dataset of IBM employees. Later on, two additional dimensions of long-term orientation, and indulgence vs. restraint were added (Hofstede et al. 2010). These dimensions have been used to explain cross-national variation in self-employment rates and innovative activities. However, the results are remarkably different based on the dependent variable, the time frame and the number of countries under investigation. For example, uncertainty avoidance is in some studies negatively correlated with inventions (e.g., Shane 1992), positively with self-employment rates (Acs et al. 1994; Hofstede et al. 2004) or not correlated with self-employment (Dheer 2017). There are inconclusive findings also for the other dimensions.

A second data source on culture across countries is the GLOBE project (House et al. 2004). Quite similar to Hofstede's approach, the respondents of the GLOBE study were managers of companies. Different from Hofstede, the GLOBE cultural dimensions of uncertainty avoidance, power distance, two versions of collectivism vs. individualism, gender egalitarism, assertiveness, future orientation, performance orientation and humane orientation were theoretically derived before data collection. The GLOBE project is also special in that it operationalizes culture in two ways as cultural values and cultural practices. While the former captures latent components of culture, the latter captures actual practices. The original GLOBE dimensions and higher order dimensions have also been repeatedly linked with entrepreneurship rates across countries without finding consistent patterns. For example, Suddle, Beugelsdijk and Wennekers (2010) found no correlation between a country's performance orientation and entrepreneurship rate. Stephan and Pathak (2016) report a significantly positive correlation between uncertainty avoidance and entrepreneurship but no statistically significant correlation between collectivism and entrepreneurship. Surprisingly, Stephan and Uhlaner (2010) do not find a relationship between the higher order GLOBE dimension of performance-based culture and entrepreneurship but report a significantly positive correlation of entrepreneurship with the socially supportive culture index.

Beside Hofstede and GLOBE, there are different datasets such as the World Value Survey and the European Values

Study from which cultural dimensions can be extracted. A promising effort exploiting these secondary data sources is the study by Beugelsdijk and Welzel (2018), who advance and validate cultural dimensions inspired by Hofstede. A different approach is taken by Schwartz (1994). Grounded in the cross-cultural psychology research field, Schwartz and his colleagues collected data on the importance of different individual values that are summarized in three cultural dimensions of autonomy versus conservatism, hierarchy vs. egalitarism, and mastery vs. harmony. However, there are few to none empirical studies at the national level regarding these datasets to evaluate their predictive ability as determinant of entrepreneurial activities. The available empirical evidence on national culture and entrepreneurship has been summarized by Hayton and Cacciotti (2013), who interpret the inconsistent findings in a rather pessimistic way: "we can be less confident, rather than more, in the existence of a single entrepreneurial culture" (p. 708). Hence, at this point it seems questionable whether concepts and research methods from cross-cultural psychology and cross-cultural research can indeed advance our understanding of the geography of entrepreneurial psychology.

Note that this rather pessimistic outlook on the concepts and measures does not mean that an entrepreneurial culture does not exist. The empirical evidence at the regional level within specific countries clearly points at the existence of such a culture that, however, differs across regions. The regional level of analysis offers some advantages over the national level to detect differences in entrepreneurship culture. Most importantly, differences in culture across regions are no longer intermingled with differences in formal institutions at the national level and are thus easier to detect. Additionally, the regional level allows case studies that compare particularly interesting regions by looking deeper into the mechanisms of how an entrepreneurial culture influences individual entrepreneurial activity. Saxenian (1996) famously compared Silicon

Valley to the region around Route 128 to find differences in values, networks, job-hopping behavior and risk-taking, among many other dimensions that differ between both regions. Greif (1994) investigated differences in cultural beliefs between medieval Genoese traders and Maghribi traders to conclude that the economic success of the former can be partly attributed to their more individualistic culture. Tabellini (2010) and Nunn and Wantchekon (2011) trace the determinants of geographic variation in trust, which is in turn a major determinant of innovation, entrepreneurship and subsequently economic growth. Davidsson (1995) and Davidsson and Wiklund (1997) find regional variation in Sweden in characteristic adaptations such as achievement orientation and locus of control that partly explain variation in entrepreneurship. The Davidsson studies, especially, stand in the tradition of the geographical psychology approach.

More indirect evidence on the presence or absence of an entrepreneurship culture is to treat observable differences in entrepreneurship rates as revealed preferences for entrepreneurship. Persistent high entrepreneurship rates in regions are then regarded as the manifestation of a latent entrepreneurial culture and vice versa (e.g., Andersson and Koster 2011; Fotopoulos and Storey 2017; Fritsch and Wyrwich 2014). This persistence phenomenon, its underlying sources and implications, are discussed in Chapter 4.

4. Persistence of regional entrepreneurship

One of the particularly important insights from recent economic research on entrepreneurial regions, and potential underlying drivers of local entrepreneurship, has to do with the so-called *persistence phenomenon* (Fritsch and Mueller 2007; Fritsch and Wyrwich 2019). This research addresses the fundamental question of spatiotemporal patterns in entrepreneurial activity and how the geography of entrepreneurial psychology could help to explain this puzzling persistence phenomenon (Obschonka et al. 2013), which would have important policy implications (see Chapter 6).

Research into the persistence of regional differences in entrepreneurial activity[1] is embedded in a wider literature that has revealed striking persistence of economic activity in general, such as certain regions that are economically more active and advanced over longer periods of time, whereas other regions continuously lag behind (e.g., Bleakley and Lin 2012; Dalgaard et al. 2018; Davis and Weinstein 2002). Such persistence is often explained by "first nature" conditions (Henderson et al. 2018) or an effect of long-lasting cultural traits among the population (for an overview, see Giuliano and Nunn 2020).

[1]   Andersson and Koster (2011); Fotopoulos (2014); Fotopoulos and Storey (2017); Fritsch and Wyrwich (2014, 2017a, 2019); Glaeser et al. (2015).

4.1   THE TENDENCY OF PERSISTENT LEVELS OF REGIONAL ENTREPRENEURSHIP

Present-day regional entrepreneurship does not start from scratch or in a social vacuum. It takes place in a certain regional and social environment that has historical roots. These historical roots constitute a particularly important determinant of regional variation in entrepreneurial activity. Studies in a number of established market economies such as West Germany, Sweden, the United Kingdom and the USA show that regional differences of start-up rates and levels of self-employment tend to be persistent over longer periods of time. A consequence of persistence of regional levels of entrepreneurial activity is that regional start-up rates[2] of successive years are highly correlated.[3] Even start-up rates across periods of more than a decade often show rather high levels of correlation. A further way to analyze such regional persistence is to compute an ordinal ranking of regions with regard to their start-up rate ('League Table') in different periods and compare the regional ranks.[4] The usual finding of such an

---

[2]   Measured as number of start-ups in a certain period divided by the number of workforce or population (Audretsch and Fritsch 1994).

[3]   Studies that demonstrate persistence of regional start-up rates have been conducted for West Germany (Fritsch and Kublina 2019; Fritsch and Mueller 2007; Fritsch and Wyrwich 2014, 2017a), the Netherlands (van Stel and Suddle 2008), Sweden (Andersson and Koster 2011), the United Kingdom (Fotopoulos 2014; Mueller et al. 2008), and for the United States (Acs and Mueller 2008).

[4]   Rank positions have several advantages over continuous metrics such as start-up rates in capturing persistence of entrepreneurship. They are not shaped by national trends of the level of entrepreneurship or by changes in the statistical reporting system. Rather, they are robust with regard to extreme cases ("outliers"), and also indicate the attractiveness of regions for entrepreneurial talent, investment and relocation of firms (Fotopoulos and Storey 2017).

approach is that these ranks are highly correlated (Fritsch and Kublina 2019).

When new business formation is used as a measure for entrepreneurship, the period of analysis is rather limited by available data. For most countries, time series on new business formation are hardly longer than 30 years. Since identifying the level of self-employment at a certain point in time is less demanding than identifying start-ups, availability of information on the level of self-employment as an indicator for entrepreneurship can cover much longer periods, sometimes more than a century. The large majority of such long-term comparisons of regional levels of self-employment identify a significant positive relationship between historical levels of self-employment and the level of entrepreneurial activity today, indicating striking long-term persistence in overall entrepreneurial activity (Fotopoulos and Storey 2017; Fritsch and Wyrwich 2014, 2019).

An obvious explanation for the persistence of regional levels of entrepreneurship could be that region-specific determinants of entrepreneurial activity also remain relatively constant over time, or, as stated by Alfred Marshall (1920), *natura non facit saltum* (nature does not make jumps). Indeed, variables that have been shown to be conducive to the emergence of new firms, such as qualifications of the regional workforce or employment share in small firms (Fritsch and Falck 2007; Sternberg 2009), do tend to remain fairly constant over successive years (Fotopoulos 2014; Fritsch and Kublina 2019). However, significant changes of the regional determinants for entrepreneurship – be it through changes of the institutional framework, in the economic environment, migration patterns or disruptive events such as wars or natural disasters – become more likely with an increasing period of analysis.

A further explanation of persistently high regional levels of new business formation is *path dependency* in the sense that current entrepreneurial activities can be regarded as a response to similar activities in a region's history (Martin and Sunley 2006). One type of such path dependency could be that high levels of new business formation create additional entrepreneurial opportunities that induce further start-ups. Another type of path dependency may result from the observation that most new ventures remain rather small (Schindele and Weyh 2011), so that high levels of start-ups lead to high shares of small business employment. Since small firms have been found to provide a more fertile seedbed for future entrepreneurs than larger firms (Elfenbein et al. 2010; Parker 2009), high levels of new business formation today may lead to correspondingly high levels of entrepreneurship in the near future via this "small firm effect".

A further mechanism that may lead to persistence of regional entrepreneurship levels is *demonstration and peer effects*. Figure 4.1 illustrates how demonstration and peer effects can induce a tendency of self-perpetuation of start-up rates, where entrepreneurial activity today induces further start-ups in the future. The main idea behind this conjecture is that an individual's perception of entrepreneurship, the cognitive representation, is shaped by observing entrepreneurial role models in the social environment (Andersson and Koster 2011; Fornahl 2003; Minniti 2005). The presence of entrepreneurial role models, particularly among one's peers, reduces ambiguity for potential entrepreneurs and may help them acquire entrepreneurial skills and necessary information (Bosma et al. 2012). It is plausible to assume that such demonstration and peer effects are particularly generated by successful founders, not by unsuccessful ones. Observing successful entrepreneurs provides potential founders with examples of how to organize resources and activities, and increases self-confidence in the sense of "if they can do it, I can, too" (Sorenson and Audia 2000, p. 443; see also e.g., Minniti 2005; Nanda and Sørenson 2010).

A self-perpetuation of regional levels of entrepreneurship can be considerably enforced if the demonstration and peer effects of many entrepreneurial role models lead to

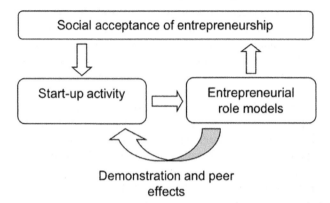

Figure 4.1   The self-perpetuation of entrepreneurship

widespread social acceptance or legitimacy (Etzioni 1987; Kibler et al. 2014) of self-employment in the local population (Figure 4.1). This may then lead to the creation of entrepreneurship-friendly framework conditions by local policymakers and a particular supportive attitude of the local administration towards private-sector firms (Westlund et al. 2014).

4.2   THE ROLE OF AN ENTREPRENEURIAL CULTURE

Research in economic geography has paid particular attention to soft regional factors as drivers of persistence in regional entrepreneurship levels. For example, research addresses the longevity of positive attitudes of the regional population towards entrepreneurship in historical constellations that are characterized by disruptive changes of the economic, social and political framework conditions. Such disruptive shocks rule out an explanation of persistence based on more or less unchanged "sticky" regional conditions for entrepreneurial activity. Persistence of entrepreneurship in the face of such disruptive changes has been studied intensely for the case of Germany (Fritsch and Wyrwich 2014, 2018, 2019). Over the course of the twentieth century, Germany experienced World War I followed by a political revolution, severe destruction in World War II, occupation by foreign countries and heavy in-migration of expellees from lost territories, 40 years of political division as a capitalist Western part and a communist Eastern section, as well as reunification of the two parts with a shock transformation of the Eastern part to a market economic system (for details, see Fritsch and Wyrwich 2019, section 3.1).

Empirical analyses of the regional levels of entrepreneurship in Germany between 1907 and today show pronounced persistence; i.e., those regions that had high levels of self-employment in the early twentieth century have a high probability of high levels of self-employment and new business formation today (Fritsch and Wyrwich 2014, 2018, 2019). It is particularly interesting in this respect that there is a highly significant positive relationship between the level of self-employment in 1925 and an entrepreneurial personality profile of today's population (Fritsch, Obschonka and Wyrwich 2019).

The 40 years of socialist administration in East Germany after World War II are of particular interest for analyzing potential drivers behind the persistence of entrepreneurship, because during this period the region was host to a significant number of policies intended to eradicate entrepreneurship. During the years of the socialist regime, collectivist values were strongly favored and entrepreneurship was perceived as a bourgeois anachronism (e.g., Pickel 1992; Thomas 1996). The implementation of a rigorous anti-entrepreneurship policy strategy included massive socialization of private enterprises and the suppression of any remaining private-sector activity (for details, see Brezinski 1987; Pickel 1992). At the end of the socialist period in 1989, the share of self-employed in the

East German population aged 18 to 64 years was only 1.8 percent, compared to about 10 percent in West Germany.

Notwithstanding the legacy effects of socialism, there was a massive surge in start-up activity in the former socialist Eastern part after the introduction of a market economy in the 1990s. During the 1990s, the self-employment rate gap between the two parts of Germany narrowed considerably and around the year 2000, the difference was no longer statistically significant. Since 2003, the level of self-employment is significantly higher in East Germany. It is particularly striking that those East German regions that had high self-employment rates at the outset of the twentieth century (before Germany was divided into a socialist regime in the East and a market economy in the West) were also those that were able to preserve relatively high self-employment rates at the end of the socialist period and showed high start-up rates thereafter (Fritsch and Wyrwich 2019; Fritsch et al. 2020a, 2021).

An explanation of persistence that may apply for periods with drastically changing framework conditions could be the presence of what economists describe as an entrepreneurial culture (Andersson and Koster 2011; Fritsch and Wyrwich 2014, 2019), which they particularly associate with a positive attitude of the population towards entrepreneurial activity that implies social legitimacy (see Chapter 3.3.2). In this view, an entrepreneurial culture is an informal institution that changes much more slowly than formal institutions, and only over rather long periods of time (North 1994; Nunn 2009; Williamson 2000). Therefore, an entrepreneurial culture should, at least to some degree, be independent of changes in the social, political and economic environment, and may even survive disruptive shocks such as devastating wars and radical transformations of political regimes (North 1994; Williamson 2000).

How such a regional culture of entrepreneurship can be transferred across generations despite severe disruptive shocks to social, political and economic framework conditions is largely unclear. A main mechanism for the transmission of an entrepreneurial spirit over time that has been well investigated in the literature is the transfer from parents to their offspring (e.g., Chlosta et al. 2012; Dohmen et al. 2012; Laspita et al. 2012; Lindquist et al. 2015). Much less is known, however, about the potential contribution of geographic mobility of people to the persistence of a regional entrepreneurial culture. If, for example, people with an entrepreneurial mindset are particularly attracted to regions that are already characterized by high levels of entrepreneurship, this supports the persistence of a regional culture of entrepreneurship. Studies for Sweden (Andersson and Koster 2011) and Germany (Fritsch and Wyrwich 2014) find that persistence of entrepreneurship can be found particularly in regions where the historical level of entrepreneurship exceeded a certain "threshold" level. This suggests that there is a critical value for the persistence and self-augmentation of a regional entrepreneurship culture.

4.3   PERSISTENCE AS RESULT OF COLLECTIVE MEMORY

The concept of collective memory has received growing multi- and interdisciplinary attention in the social sciences since the millennium, involving disciplines such as sociology, psychology, history, philosophy and anthropology (Olick 1999; Roediger and DeSoto 2014; Hirst, Yamashiro and Coman 2018). It lends itself as a promising approach that could help explain the persistence phenomenon of entrepreneurship for the following reasons.

Similar to the historical patterns of entrepreneurship identified in Germany, persistence of entrepreneurship despite a number of disruptive shocks has also been confirmed for the case of Poland (Fritsch, Pylak and Wyrwich 2019) and for the area of Kaliningrad (Fritsch et al. 2019). Kaliningrad represents an extreme example of long-term persistent entrepreneurship where the rather disruptive changes included not only more than 40 years of a communist regime where private economic activity was illegal, but also a complete exchange of the local population.[5] Fritsch et al.'s empirical analysis revealed that the levels of self-employment per industry in the sub-regions of the Kaliningrad area in 1925 contribute significantly to explaining the regional levels of self-employment today. Hence, those sub-regions with relatively high (low) levels of entrepreneurship in 1925 also show relatively high (low) levels of self-employment today.

A quite similar case is the Polish region of Silesia that was German until World War II and fell to Poland afterwards (Fritsch, Pylak and Wyrwich 2019). Also in this case, the original German population was expelled after the war and substituted by people of Polish nationality. In the 1920s, Silesia was a relatively competitive region with high shares of manufacturing employment and particularly high levels of self-employment in knowledge-intensive manufacturing industries. Comparing regional levels of self-employment in the sub-regions of Silesia in the 1920s with the levels of entrepreneurship in current periods shows significant correspondence so that sub-regions with high (low) levels of self-employment in knowledge-intensive manufacturing show generally high (low) levels of self-employment today.[6] The

---

[5] The Kaliningrad region was German territory until the end of World War II, and then became part of Russia with a socialist planned economy where any form of private economic activity was illegal until the economic reforms in the early 1990s. After World War II, the Russian authorities completely expelled the original German population of Kaliningrad and replaced them with people from other regions of the Soviet Union. These changes, as well as heavy destruction during the war, rule out that persistence of entrepreneurship is driven by sticky regional characteristics or was due to a transfer of entrepreneurial values, attitudes and abilities across generations, from parents to their offspring.

[6] A further example could be regions in West Germany where expellees from former German territories that were placed there after World War II led to a strong increase in population numbers.

persistence of regional entrepreneurship found in the regions of Kaliningrad and Silesia is rather remarkable because – due to the exchange of the local population – persistence of entrepreneurship in these territories cannot be based, at least in these specific cases, on an intergenerational transmission of personality traits and entrepreneurial attitudes. There must have been something else that caused the persistence in these regions.

Based on the cases of the Kaliningrad area and Silesia, Fritsch et al. (2019) introduce a general awareness of the regional entrepreneurial history or a "collective memory" as a further potential explanation for persistence of entrepreneurship. Put differently, a collective memory of the historical experience of relatively high levels of entrepreneurship could have triggered the re-emergence of entrepreneurship after a more than 40-year lapse, during which time private economic activity was suppressed by the political regime. Fritsch et al. (2019) argue that the collective memory may have been induced by knowledge of local firms and industries that existed in prewar times and were obvious to the incoming population in the form of the physical remains of buildings and infrastructure, or known from documents and common narratives (Olick, Vinitzky-Seroussi and Levy 2011). The pre-existing industry and firm size structures may have given the new citizens an indication of the type of economic activity for which the place-specific endowments are particularly suitable. After the dissolution of the communist regime, the collective memory of entrepreneurship may have become activated, and encouraged people to start their own companies. Based on their empirical results, Fritsch et al. (2019) and Fritsch, Pylak and Wyrwich (2019) conjecture that it is particularly successful historical entrepreneurship that is important for persistence.

4.4   PERSISTENT ENTREPRENEURSHIP AND ECONOMIC DEVELOPMENT

Several studies indicate that long-term persistence of high levels of entrepreneurship, which may indicate a persisting regional culture or a collective memory of entrepreneurship, is conducive to economic growth and to the recovery from disruptive events such as devastating wars or economic crises. Glaeser, Pekkala-Kerr and Kerr (2015) use the geographic distance to coal mines around the year 1900 as an instrument for historical entrepreneurship. Since coal mining and related industries (e.g., steel) are typically large-scale activities, the authors assume that proximity to coal mines indicates low levels of entrepreneurship and a respective entrepreneurial culture (see also Chapter 5.2.1). They find a positive effect of distance to the nearest historical coal mine on growth in the 1982–2002 period.

Fritsch and Wyrwich (2017a, 2019) use the share of self-employed persons in the regional 1925 workforce as measure for historical entrepreneurship in Germany and find that West German regions with high levels of historical self-employment tend to have more start-ups at the outset of their period of analysis (1975) and higher employment growth. Their analysis indicates that the positive relationship between new business formation and employment growth is more pronounced in regions with a historically grounded culture of entrepreneurship. Fritsch, Obschonka and Wyrwich (2019) show a distinct and statistically significant positive relationship between the historical self-employment levels in 1925 and innovative activities today as indicated by the share of R&D personnel, start-ups in innovative industries and patent applications per population. Analyzing economic development in East German regions after German unification in the 1989–2018 period, Fritsch and Wyrwich (2020) find that regions with high levels of self-employment at the end of the socialist period in 1989 were considerably better able to cope with the challenges of the shock transformation from a planned socialist system to a market economy, and showed the highest growth rates.

4.5   SUMMARY: WHY IS REGIONAL ENTREPRENEURSHIP SO PERSISTENT?

Long-term persistence of regional entrepreneurship has been identified rather recently when information on regional self-employment in earlier times and longer time series became more freely available. Correspondence of regional self-employment levels about a century ago with current levels is particularly fascinating and deserves explanation.

Persistence of entrepreneurship within relatively stable framework conditions is perhaps explained by the intergenerational transfer of firms, resources and particularly personality traits and individual values of the local population. Some scholars also speculate whether personality traits and values of the local population may represent a culture of entrepreneurship that can survive disruptive shocks such as devastating wars or complete changes of the institutional framework (Fritsch and Wyrwich 2014, 2017a, 2019). The local intergeneration transmission of such traits and values can be excluded as an explanation of the persistence phenomenon in regions where the local population has been more or less completely exchanged, as was the case in the areas of Kaliningrad (Fritsch et al. 2019) and Silesia (Fritsch, Pylak and Wyrwich 2019) after World War II.

However, regional psychological factors could still matter in such regions, even if local intergeneration transmission can be ruled out. One mechanism at work in such a setting could be selective migration, when places that have an image of being particularly entrepreneurial attract migrants with an entrepreneurial mindset. In that case, selective influx of particularly entrepreneurially minded people to a place

where the former population was also more entrepreneurially minded could lead to persistence of the entrepreneurial
macro-psychological profile. Also the (collective) migration
experience itself can have the potential to shape the (collective) personality of the immigrating population (Lönnqvist et
al. 2011). One could also ask whether the collective migration
experience could create a local identity and narrative as a collective memory of human (entrepreneurial) agency associated
with the immigration and "starting a new life". Finally, the
local industry structure could contribute to a persistence in the
macro-psychological profile in these regions when both the
populations that left and moved into these regions developed
a more entrepreneurial culture as a result of work experiences
in specific types of industries and company structures conducive to an entrepreneurship culture (Stuetzer et al. 2016).

Taken together, one way of interpreting the persistence of
entrepreneurship that is found in regions where large parts
of the local population were exchanged is by going back to
Marshall's (1920) notion that there might be "something in
the air" that drives economic mechanisms. This could be
the regional personality structure and a collective memory
of a region's economic history that is triggered by physical
remains, documents or narratives of earlier entrepreneurship.

To conclude, the fascinating existing research on the striking persistence of regional entrepreneurial activity that one
can identify over such longer periods of time delivers important food for thought for the geography of entrepreneurial psychology. This is even more relevant since there is a growing
body of empirical evidence looking at the historical origins
(and persistence) of regional psychological factors associated
with entrepreneurship – the next chapter will provide an overview of this research.

5. Historical roots

5.1 DYNAMIC PERSPECTIVES

One of the fascinating new topics that results from studying the geography of entrepreneurial psychology as well as the persistence phenomenon of entrepreneurship concerns the origins of present-day regional differences in entrepreneurial psychological characteristics. As illustrated in Chapter 4, examining the historical origins of a region's entrepreneurship levels (e.g., why have some regions emerged and persisted as entrepreneurial hotspots?) has become an important research focus (Fritsch and Wyrwich 2019; Glaeser et al. 2015; for an overview, see also Fritsch and Storey 2014). The reason for this interest is to learn more about historical forms and effects of entrepreneurship (Casson and Casson 2014; Landes et al. 2010) and particularly recognition that the underlying regional drivers of present-day entrepreneurship might go far back in history, with important historical roots that continue to shape the economic and social trajectories of regions today and may well do so in the future (Acemoglu and Robinson 2012; Nunn 2009, 2012).

One of the drivers of present-day entrepreneurship in a region is arguably the regional psychological make-up as indicated by the growing body of empirical evidence studying the geography of entrepreneurial psychology. For example, one can ask where the regional differences arise between the US Rust Belt and the American West in terms of an entrepreneurship-prone personality profile (Obschonka et al. 2013). Why are certain regions collectively more entrepreneurially minded than others? Are there particularly influential events and epochs in history that have left such a deep macro-psychological imprint in regions that this is still shaping the behavior of local populations today? These are very complex questions that concern fundamental changes in society and regions over longer periods of time – decades and centuries – including historical migration patterns, technological developments and socioeconomic shocks, but also the persistence phenomenon in regional entrepreneurship (Fritsch and Wyrwich 2014, 2019).

What is obviously needed to address these questions is an interdisciplinary approach, particularly a combination of psychology, economics, human geography and history. Such research endeavors go beyond a simple "psychological archaeology" – a study of the historical artifacts and structures that might be sometimes deeply hidden under the rubble of ancient or more recent societies and institutions. It would inform our general understanding of the emergence, persistence and manifestation of geographical variation in entrepreneurial psychology (Rentfrow et al. 2008) that is important for theory building and policymaking and which has practical implications for present-day societies and regions.

5.2   HISTORICAL INDUSTRY STRUCTURE

One major historical factor that is likely to shape the geography of entrepreneurial psychology in a profound way is the historical industry structure in a region and the form of self-employment, even if these industries or forms of self-employment have lost their dominance and influence in the region (Abdellaoui et al. 2019; Obschonka et al. 2018; Talhelm et al. 2014). So far, empirical analyses have identified respective peculiarities for large-scale industries (Section 5.2.1), agriculture and homeworkers (Section 5.2.2) as well as for industries that can be regarded as science-based (Section 5.2.3).

5.2.1   Large-scale industries

Stuetzer et al. (2016) put this idea of an industrial heritage that contributed to present-day macro-psychological patterns that underlie entrepreneurship to an empirical test. The authors investigated regions that were significantly shaped by the Industrial Revolution (generally acknowledged as the period *c.*1760 to *c.*1840) that transformed society first in the UK and then in many other countries through an unprecedented massive increase in manufacturing, particularly in large-scale industries such as textile production, metal manufacturing, bricks and pottery, and mining. In the UK, these large-scale industries were often concentrated in regions with proximity to coalfields since coal powered the steam engines that then provided the energy to run the large factories. Due to the relatively high transportation costs for coal in the UK at that time, the establishment of these economic centers near coalfields was a very rational decision. Entirely new agglomeration centers emerged around coalfields due to the massive influx of workers with their families and the concentration of people and manufacturing activities in these regions. They became economic powerhouses and even today these old industrial centers remain significant population hubs in many countries shaped by the Industrial Revolution (e.g., the UK, the USA and Germany). However, many of these former economic powerhouses have endured a strong economic slump over the past 50 years or so – a downturn that went hand in hand with a decline in these large-scale industries that had left such a major imprint in these regions.

Stuetzer et al.'s (2016) study was guided by economic theorizing on the detrimental effects of large-scale industries on collective entrepreneurial characteristics of local populations. The economist Benjamin Chinitz (1961) had hypothesized that regional differences in entrepreneurial activity across the USA (e.g., between New York and Pittsburgh) have to do with the industrial–cultural imprint in these regions. Chinitz (1961) argued that large-scale capital intensive production in large firms was less conducive to entrepreneurship because the culture, attitudes and values of the personnel were not conducive to initiative, independent decision-making and risk-taking that are key elements of entrepreneurial behavior. By contrast, the high prevalence of independent and autonomous small businesses in New York was more conducive to entrepreneurial attitudes and cultures. In particular, Chinitz (1961) argued that because of the large-scale structure of the Pittsburgh economy there were fewer independent business owners with the experience and capabilities to transfer entrepreneurial values and attitudes to the next generation of potential entrepreneurs, which in turn would lead to persisting lower levels of entrepreneurship.

This notion of a cultural imprint of a local concentration of large-scale industries is reminiscent of a socialization perceptive in entrepreneurial psychology, where the nature of work, including single work tasks and actions (Frese 1982; Frese and Gielnik 2014), as well as the associated local norms and habits in a region, shape the entrepreneurial mindset of persons living and working in these regions (Talhelm et al. 2014). While this seems a plausible assumption, selective migration patterns (e.g., outflux of entrepreneurially minded people) should play an important role as well (Abdellaoui et al. 2019; Obschonka et al. 2018) – which follows more the selection perspective in entrepreneurial psychology where relatively stable personality traits are an important component of the entrepreneurial mindset and shape entrepreneurial thinking and acting of a person rather than the other way around. When such entrepreneurial personality patterns concentrate at the regional level they exert arguably region-level effects on entrepreneurial thinking and acting of local populations via local norms, attitudes and role models. Hence, one way how the Industrial Revolution might have contributed to the geographic differentiation in entrepreneurial psychology is through several waves of selective migration patterns, including the outflux of more entrepreneurially minded people who searched for a more entrepreneurial regional environment.

There are also economic mechanisms in how large-scale industries are detrimental to entrepreneurship (Glaeser et al. 2015). Stuetzer et al. (2016) note that large-scale industries are characterized by a pronounced division of labor. Many employees have specialized jobs which limit the range of practical skills they can acquire. Looking back at the Industrial Revolution, the large-scale textile industry was among the first to use assembly line production techniques, reducing workers to performing repetitive manual tasks. In contrast, in small firms with less division of labor, employees engage in a multitude of tasks and consequently acquire a diverse set of skills quite frequently through learning by doing (e.g., Elfenbein et al. 2010; Wagner 2004).

This difference in skill-sets has important consequences for entrepreneurship. Lazear (2005) introduced the notion that entrepreneurs, especially in the start-up phase, need to be jack-of-all-trades because most start-up projects are solo endeavors and in case of team start-ups seldom involve more than three people. Beside pure practical skills, employees in small firms tend to have regular contact with the firm's owner, providing direct contact to an entrepreneurial role model. Such contact is largely missing in large-scale firms where the average employee rarely knows the entrepreneur. In short, small firms can be regarded as a breeding ground for entrepreneurs (Mueller 2006; Parker 2009). Scaled to the regional level, regions that are dominated by large-scale industries with employees lacking skills and contact with entrepreneurial role models cannot be expected to produce many entrepreneurs.

Regarding the long-term effects of the Industrial Revolution, it is noteworthy that the once dominating industries such as textile and steel are of much less importance today than they were some centuries ago. The last deep coal mine in the UK was closed in 2016, textile production has been outsourced to Southeast Asia and the steel industry has rapidly declined. Naturally, the question arises how this industrial history still matters for today's entrepreneurship.

As was discussed in greater detail in Chapter 4, there is a pronounced persistence in regional entrepreneurship rates over time (e.g., Andersson and Koster 2011; Fritsch and Wyrwich 2014). One explanation for this persistence (highlighted in Chapter 4) was the presence or absence of regional entrepreneurship cultures of which the regional pattern of entrepreneurial personality traits is arguably a major component. The Industrial Revolution provides one case in point how industry structure can influence personality traits. Once regions were dominated by large-scale firms, leading to an entrepreneurship-inhibiting mindset in the regional populace and reduced entrepreneurial activities, a vicious cycle is set in motion. The entrepreneurship-inhibiting mindset discourages people from engaging in entrepreneurship (Etzioni 1987) and the resulting scarceness of entrepreneurial role models further weakens the entrepreneurial mindset in a region's population (Fritsch and Wyrwich 2017b). This cycle is self-reinforcing and leads to low regional entrepreneurship and innovation, even more than 200 years after the original determinant of the rise of large-scale industries of the Industrial Revolution have vanished.

Empirical evidence regarding the relationship between the historical industry structure, on the one hand, and entrepreneurial personality characteristics and activities, on the other hand, can be visualized easily. Figure 5.1 (A) presents the geographic distribution of nineteenth-century coalfields in the UK. The regions with coal or those close to coalfields enjoyed lower coal prices because, as a bulky commodity, it was expensive to transport (B). Consequently, the energy-dependent large-scale industries such as textile and metal manufacturing were located in these regions. Map (C) in Figure 5.1 shows that in some parts of Britain, such as the Midlands, South Wales and mid-Scotland, between 25 percent and 60 percent of the regional workforce was employed in these industries. Conversely, in coal-less regions, coal prices were high and the employment share of these energy-dependent large-scale industries was negligible. The long-term impact on entrepreneurial activity and an entrepreneurial mindset is displayed in Figure 5.2, which shows less entrepreneurial personality patterns (A), lower self-employment rates (B), and lower start-up rates (C) in the same parts of Britain in which the large-scale industries

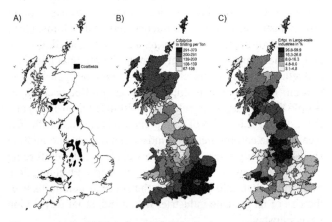

Note: A) Coalfields before 1700; B) coal prices around 1840; and C) 1891 employment share in large-scale industries. The measure of employment in large-scale industries refers to employment in textiles, metal manufacturing, bricks and pottery, and coal mining.
Source: Data are taken from the 1891 Census (https://www .nationalarchives.gov.uk/). Updated analysis at Local Authority District (LAD) level from Stuetzer et al. (2016).

Figure 5.1   Coal and employment in large-scale industries during the Industrial Revolution

dominated. While the effect of a vicious cycle of missing
entrepreneurial mindsets and entrepreneurial activities might
have been eroded somewhat over time, the anti-entrepreneurial values, norms and personality profiles remain deeply
seated in these regions (Abdellaoui et al. 2019; Stuetzer et al.
2016) and will probably aggravate an economic revival via
entrepreneurship and innovation.

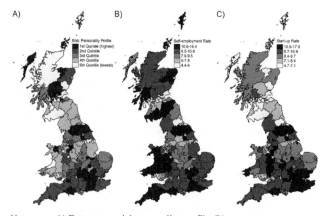

Note: A) Entrepreneurial personality profile; B) average
self-employment rate 2004–11; and C) average start-up rate 2004–11. The
start-up rates are computed as the number of business births per 1,000
employees. The self-employment rates are computed by the number of
self-employed over the working-age population.
Source: The personality data are taken from the BBC Lab Project (no
longer available). Data on self-employment are taken from the Office for
National Statistics (ONS) (https://www.ons.gov.uk/). Data on start-ups are
taken from the Inter-Departmental Business Register (IDBR) (https://www
.ons.gov.uk/aboutus/whatwedo/paidservices/interdepartmentalbusinessre
gisteridbr). Updated analysis based on Stuetzer et al. (2016).

*Figure 5.2   Entrepreneurial personality profile and
entrepreneurship rates in British Local
Authority Districts (LADs)*

5.2.2   Farmers and homeworkers

Fritsch, Obschonka and Wyrwich (2019) analyzed the relationships between historical levels of self-employment, personality traits of the regional population, current levels of new business formation and innovation activity across German regions. The authors find a positive and statistically significant relationship between the level of regional self-employment in 1925 and the entrepreneurial personality profile of today's population as measured by the Big Five if they exclude self-employment in agriculture (farmers) and homeworkers. Running the analysis separately for farmers and homeworkers does not show any long-lasting entrepreneurial imprinting effect on the entrepreneurial personality profile of the local population. This corresponds to the finding that historical levels of self-employment in agriculture and the share of homeworkers are not related to regional new business formation today (Fritsch and Wyrwich 2016b).

An explanation for the non-significance of homeworkers for persistence of entrepreneurship could be that they represent a marginal and mainly necessity-driven form of self-employment that can hardly be regarded as a successful role model. Homeworkers in the 1920s often produced goods or performed few and often simple manufacturing steps for one single final producer or retailer. Although homeworkers may be regarded as "freelancers", the vast majority of them were closely integrated into the production processes of their principal firm and had low levels of economic self-determination. Moreover, they did not perform many of the tasks, such as marketing, management, etc., that characterize entrepreneurship. Hence, they fall midway between an independent entrepreneur and a dependent employee.

Also, agriculture constitutes a rather special case that is hardly comparable to other industries. In particular, it requires qualifications and abilities that differ considerably from entrepreneurship in other sectors. One special feature of self-employment in agriculture in early twentieth-century Germany was that farms in most German regions consisted almost entirely of family businesses that were passed on by customs of inheritance. Hence, hardly any farm owner had to experience the risky process of founding and establishing his or her business. Moreover, since growth of farms was limited by available acreage, business strategies of farmers were dominated by attempts to preserve their farms; expansion played a rather minor role, if any. In contrast, self-employment in non-agricultural sectors of the economy is much more critically related to industrialization and economic development. Therefore, it more positively reflects perceived role models and is more closely associated with the generation of additional entrepreneurial opportunities than self-employment in agriculture.

5.2.3   Science-based industries

Entrepreneurship in science-based or knowledge-intensive industries may leave a more important imprint on the attitude of the regional population towards self-employment and have a stronger effect on the persistence of regional entrepreneurship than self-employment in other industries. Generally, self-employment in science-based industries requires a specific set of entrepreneurial abilities and qualifications that frequently include pronounced knowledge in natural sciences and engineering (Fritsch and Aamoucke 2017). Moreover, they tend to be more innovative and create more additional entrepreneurial opportunities that may be adopted by other firms and stimulate start-ups. Hence, the self-employed in science-based industries are likely to represent a rather positive role model of successful entrepreneurship.

Regions with a high share of historical entrepreneurship in science-based industries tend to have more historical examples of successful entrepreneurs that can serve as attractive role models. Thus, high historical levels of science-based entrepreneurship should make a particular positive imprint on the attitudes of the regional population towards entrepreneurship and should also facilitate the prevalence of a place-based collective memory that can stimulate new business formation many years later.

Fritsch, Obschonka and Wyrwich (2019) found that the effect of historical self-employment in science-based industries on the entrepreneurial personality fit in today's German regions is at least as strong as for the overall historical level of self-employment. Investigating the determinants of science-based entrepreneurship, Fritsch and Wyrwich (2019) found a positive effect of geographic proximity to universities, particularly to universities of technology.

5.3   INSTITUTIONS

Beside historical industry structures, institutions can also be a major historical factor shaping the geography of entrepreneurial psychology. Institutions are often defined as the rules of the game comprising formal laws but also informal norms and conventions such as cultures and traditions (Baumol 1990; North 1994). Both formal and informal institutions shape individual behavior and, in the aggregate, regional personality characteristics. Institutions can have a normative influence on personality characteristics in a rather direct way via socialization. Children born into a specific set of formal institutions are often raised in a way not to get in conflict with the institutional setting but rather to fit in. Later on, state-influenced educational systems also shape thinking patterns of pupils to match the existing set of institutions. Collectively, formal and informal institutions affect experiences and opportunities within regions and countries that in turn influence psychological and behavioral tendencies of the populace (Rentfrow et al. 2008).

The effect of institutions on entrepreneurial psychology is a rather under-researched field. A main focus of available studies is the effect of communism on personality characteristics relevant for people's entrepreneurial intentions and their subsequent actions to become an entrepreneur. In Chapter 2.4, we discussed the entrepreneurial personality system and described the differences between the rather stable personality traits such as the Big Five and the characteristic adaptations such as fear of failure and risk-taking that are more prone to change. In the following paragraphs we focus on the effect of communism on such characteristic adaptations.

Cantoni et al.'s (2017) study investigates the effect of curriculum change in China. While China has been under the rule of the Communist Party from 1949, its stance toward the market system has changed over time. With the economic reforms starting in the late 1970s, China incorporated elements of the market system allowing entrepreneurship and focusing on economic growth. Starting from 2001, however, new textbooks for high school students were introduced that again strongly emphasize the importance of the socialist market economy and reject the notion of free markets. Interestingly, the introduction of the textbook varies across Chinese provinces, allowing Cantoni et al. (2017) to estimate causal effects of this ideological change on attitudes regarding the market system and individual risk-taking. The results show that Chinese students under the new curriculum are more skeptical of markets and are less likely to be invested in bonds and stocks (more risk-aversion) compared to students taught under the old curriculum.

Wyrwich et al.'s (2016) study exploits the division of Germany and later unification. East Germany was marked by four decades of socialism while West Germany was an established market economy. With reunification the complete setting of formal institutions in East Germany was abolished and West German formal institutions adopted. The question Wyrwich et al. (2016) asks is whether the socialist legacy has left an imprint on one particular personality characteristic relevant for entrepreneurship: fear of failure. Fear of failure belongs to the group of characteristic adaptations that is not as stable as personality traits and thus is inexorable to ideology as well as economic and political institutional constraints. Fear of failure is detrimental to entrepreneurship because few people engage in an activity when they fear the economic and psychological consequences of failing in this activity.

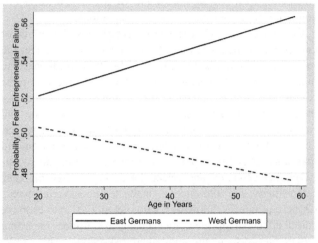

Note: Fear of failure is measured with the question whether or not fear of failure would prevent the respondent starting up a new business.
Source: The data are taken from the 2003–08 German Global Entrepreneurship Monitor (GEM) survey (no website available). Updated analysis based on Wyrwich et al. (2016).

Figure 5.3   Probability of the fear of entrepreneurial failure among East and West Germans

With respect to entrepreneurship there are good reasons to fear failure because failing in terms of financial losses depletes available economic resources, and leads to grief and shame about the failure and stigmatization from others (Jenkins et al. 2014). These effects might be more pronounced in East Germany where institutions were detrimental to entrepreneurship and socialist indoctrination painted a picture of the entrepreneur as an exploiter of labor. Indeed, the results using German GEM data show that East Germans fear more entrepreneurial failure compared to West Germans. This difference is smallest among younger people but gets steadily stronger in older age cohorts, which makes sense as older people were more exposed to socialist indoctrination and institutions (Figure 5.3). Even the presence of entrepreneurial role models that should lead to a reduction of fear of failure has no significant effect on older East Germans.

5.4 DEEPER CULTURAL IMPRINTS

Finally, historical research addressing the geography of entre-preneurial psychology might not only find it promising to look at major historical events and radical changes that have occurred since the Industrial Revolution around 200 years ago, but could even consider major societal transformations underway much earlier in human history. There is broad consensus that influential historical processes shaping local collective mindsets can reach far back in time (Becker and Woessmann 2009; Boyd and Richerson 2005; Nunn 2009, 2012; Schulz et al. 2019) – many centuries or even millennia ago – with a potentially very deep and persisting imprinting effect that is still detectable in psychological characteristics and corresponding behaviors of today's regional populations.

Fritsch et al. (2020c) examine how a major societal trans-formation in the pre-industrial era, Roman rule in some parts of Germany nearly 2,000 years ago, might have left a deep cultural imprint that shaped the geography of entrepreneurial psychology until today. At first glance, it might seem unlikely that such a distant historical factor could continue to have an effect on entire modern-day psychological landscapes, par-ticularly if one takes into account the many disruptive changes that the German regions have experienced over the centuries, such as in- and out-migration of population, devastating wars and diseases, changing administrative borders and political regimes, changing religions, as well as – last but not least – enormous developments in technology and social practices, and a pronounced increase in economic welfare.

When combining present-day macro-psychological data with historical data reaching back to the Roman empire, Fritsch et al.'s (2020c) study indeed provides evidence for a statistically significant relationship between being part of the Roman Empire nearly 2,000 years ago and regional personality traits associated with entrepreneurship (the entre-preneurial Big Five profile; see Obschonka et al. 2013; Schmitt-Rodermund 2004, 2007). This relationship remains relatively robust when controlling for a number of alterna-tive explanations such as locational characteristics, climate, quality of the soil, the number of plague outbreaks in the Middle Ages or being a main center of Roman trade. The authors assume and test the idea that enduring advancements in physical infrastructure conducive to trade, economic pros-perity and the exchange of ideas and new knowledge might be a relevant mechanism why Roman rule had contributed to the establishment and persistence of these more entrepreneurial regional personality characteristics, compared to German regions that were not part of the Roman Empire (e.g., the former regions of the Germanic barbarians).

Fritsch et al. (2020c) find solid indications that the density of the road network that the Romans had established in Southern Germany plays an important role. This had an influ-ence on the level of interregional mobility and the geography of social and economic interactions. In particular, higher levels of mobility and interregional interactions could very likely affect population attitudes towards strangers, its level of risk aversion and tolerance towards change, and its open-ness to new ideas. Roman roads also connected this part of Germany with other parts of the Roman Empire. Hence, this road network could have helped to establish a certain early civilization advantage in these German regions, compared to the less developed "barbaric" cultures north of the Limes Germanicus – the old Roman frontier fortifications. Besides the Roman road network, the authors also found some indication that the presence of Roman markets and mines, places with relatively high levels of economic and social activity, could have been important for the deep cultural imprinting effect of the Romans in Germany. High economic and social activity levels may have created pronounced incentives for creativity and innovativeness and may, therefore, have attracted people with such traits to these places.

The authors have also studied regional advantages in knowledge production and dissemination of new knowledge in the former Roman regions in Germany during medieval times. They found that Roman rule, and particularly the Roman road network, is associated with more knowledge and economic activity in this historical era (e.g., number of students 1458–1508, number of books pre-1517, number of markets in 1470, share of economic buildings 1400–1600). Hence, one explanation of a persisting historical imprint of Roman rule and associated cultural and economic advances almost 2,000 years ago in Southern Germany could be that Roman society established knowledge spillover institutions that persisted over time. We know that in today's modern economy, knowledge and particularly knowledge spillovers are key competitive advantages of (entrepreneurial) regions (Acs et al. 2009).

6. Implications for practice, education and policy

6.1 IMPLICATIONS FOR PRACTICE

The growing knowledge on geographical aspects of entrepreneurial psychology still represents a rather small field and implications can only be preliminary at this point – more research is required to come to robust conclusions with clear implications for practice. However, a few emerging implications for practice are worth noting.

One potentially important implication for entrepreneurs and entrepreneurial practice deals with the notion that the place-component of entrepreneurship (e.g., *where* budding entrepreneurs start their new businesses) is embedded in a macro-psychological context that differs across places and regions, and which interacts with the entrepreneur and his/her business in various ways. Start-ups do not emerge and operate in a vacuum but, besides economic factors, there is also an important psychological context.

Moreover, entrepreneurs could incorporate such a macro-psychological perspective and insights into self-reflective processes, for example those related to the crystallization of their occupational self-concept (e.g., self-identity), which is an important component of the entrepreneurial personality system (Fauchart and Gruber 2011; Hoang and Gimeno 2010; Obschonka 2016; Obschonka and Stuetzer 2017) – and, in general, an important developmental factor in vocational development over the life course

(Savickas 2002; Super 1963). The notion that the place where budding entrepreneurs grew up can also have a deep psychological imprint on their personality, which in turn shapes their entrepreneurial mindset, can help entrepreneurs to reflect on their own identity, and why they might view and interpret the world in various ways. Many biographies of entrepreneurs tell anecdotal stories about how important the psychological and physical place of their childhood and teenage years was. These early formative years shape personality and thus also the entrepreneurial mindset which has been demonstrated in a variety of studies (Geldhof et al. 2014; Obschonka 2016; Obschonka et al. 2011a, 2011b; Schmitt-Rodermund 2004, 2007; Schoon and Duckworth 2012). One of the strongest lessons from skill formation and human capital research is how important these early formative years, early experiences and skill formation are as development factors that determine success later in life (Cunha et al. 2006; Heckman 2006; Masten et al. 2010).

Moreover, in their daily practice of starting and running a business, an evidence-based understanding of the local macro-psychological climate and mechanisms could help entrepreneurs in their decision-making. This could, for example, concern how to deal with local attitudes, norms and values. Many entrepreneurs face challenges around legitimacy and market acceptance with their new businesses (Kibler and Kautonen 2016) and a better understanding of the local psychology of the business environment could help them to gain more legitimacy and acceptance (more quickly) – for example, by resonating with local attitudes, norms and values. Another important example is innovation adoption. It seems important for entrepreneurs to consider that the local macro-psychology should also affect openness in local markets to adopt new products and services – the appetite for vs. resistance to innovation. Entrepreneurs could consider the specific macro-psychological profile of a given place or region where their business operates from an innovation adoption perspective. However, much more research is needed to shed light on the role of macro-psychological factors for innovation adoption and diffusion in the context of entrepreneurship.

6.2   IMPLICATIONS FOR EDUCATION

Entrepreneurial education (e.g., enterprise and entrepreneurship education; see Quality Assurance Agency 2012) has become an important strategy in societies around the world not only to develop future generations of successful entrepreneurs (Fayolle 2018), but also, more broadly, to help in equipping young generations with new meta-skills (Bellanca 2010; Griffin and Care 2014) needed to succeed in life and in their careers (Huber et al. 2014; Obschonka et al. 2017). What are the potential implications coming from existing research on geographical aspects of entrepreneurial psychology for the field of entrepreneurial education?

First, growing empirical evidence revealing existing regional variations in relatively basic and stable entrepreneurial psychological characteristics such as the entrepreneurial Big Five profile can have concrete implications for the education field. Understood as basic tendencies in the entrepreneurial personality system (Obschonka and Stuetzer 2017), these traits represent biologically related propensities in a person's entrepreneurial development over the life-span (Obschonka 2016). Obschonka and Stuetzer (2017) describe and show a gravity effect of these basic tendencies in a person's entrepreneurial personality system; they shape the development of characteristics adaptions (e.g., specific entrepreneurial traits like self-efficacy, risk-taking or internal locus of control) as well as the development of an entrepreneurial concept (e.g., entrepreneurial self-identity; Obschonka et al. 2015).

Consistent with the Five-Factor Theory (FFT) Personality System model (McCrae and Costa 2008), such basic tendencies represent the enduring core of a person's personality system; a core that guides the learning and adaption processes via characteristic interactions with the environment over the person's life-span (see also McAdams and Pals 2006). This means that these basic tendencies basically shape the whole course of the growth and development of the entrepreneurial mindset and how the individual interacts and learns from the environment, including entrepreneurial education. Educational programs should therefore consider such a differential perspective as not every student has the same basic entrepreneurial personality structure. Students within the classroom may differ, but, more importantly from the perspective of this book, students may differ across places and regions. In other words, educators should be aware of such regional differences and they could consider using a tailored approach informed by empirical evidence on the local macro-psychological profile.

For example, in regions with a higher likelihood that the average student shows a less entrepreneurial basic personality structure than the average student in other regions (e.g., in old industrial centers as indicated in some studies; see Obschonka et al. 2013; Stuetzer et al. 2016), educational programs aiming to develop entrepreneurial mindsets might have to be particularly intensive and long term, and might need to start early in life (e.g., primary school) to achieve a significant, enduring effect (Obschonka and Stuetzer 2017). On the other hand, in regions with a collectively more entrepreneurial personality structure, educational programs might be more of a trigger of latent entrepreneurial interests and talents in students, particularly if the student has not come into contact with entrepreneurship before due to the absence of entrepreneurial role models (Schröder and Schmitt-Rodermund 2006).

However, it is important to note that these are still preliminary implications and we need much more research, also in the classroom and studies following whole student cohorts into their occupation career (Schmitt-Rodermund 2007; Schmitt-Rodermund et al. 2019; Schoon and Duckworth 2012). So far empirical evidence is very mixed whether existing educational programs work or not (e.g., Huber et al. 2014; Oosterbeek et al. 2010), indicating that more needs to be done to improve the effectiveness of such programs. A geographical entrepreneurship psychology perspective could deliver important insights in how to improve such programs by considering the local macro-psychological context that may shape entrepreneurial learning.

Second, the field of entrepreneurial education should not only look at place-related likelihoods of entrepreneurial personality characteristics in local student populations; the same could apply to teachers and their personality structure (Murray et al. 1990). Given that teachers, and their entrepreneurial mindsets can play an important role for the effectiveness of entrepreneurial education (Ruskovaara and Pihkala 2015; Seikkula-Leino et al. 2010), their own entrepreneurial personality structure could make a difference. We can only speculate, but it could be, for example, that in regions where the local (student) population shows a less entrepreneurial personality structure, it might require a particularly entrepreneurial teacher to boost educational success in this field. However, again, more research is needed to put such potential implications to an empirical test. But we deem it important that such macro-psychological thinking enters educational institutions, to at least consider and discuss recent advances in the research field.

Third, we deem it important, from an ethical perspective, that the field of entrepreneurial education does not misinterpret research findings on the geography of entrepreneurial psychology. We know, for example, that such basic personality traits have an effect on the development of the entrepreneurial mindset (e.g., Obschonka et al. 2017; Schmitt-Rodermund 2004, 2007), but this effect is not very large and should not be misinterpreted as being deterministic. For example, it would, of course, be incorrect to assume that only students with such a personality structure can become entrepreneurs – because such traits and underlying biological components can be better interpreted as propensities in a person's development, instead of factors that strictly predetermine a person's development (Gottlieb 2007; Obschonka 2016). Also, students scoring lower in an entrepreneurial personality structure can have an entrepreneurial mindset, and vice versa.

Entrepreneurship as a developmental outcome is characterized by equifinality – this means different starting points in a person's development can lead to the same outcome, such as starting and running a successful business. Equifinality (and multifinality, where the same starting point leads to different development outcomes) are fundamental principles of human development (Cicchetti and Rogosch 1996). Moreover, the field of epigenetics has delivered important new insights in how biologically related factors in human development not only shape developmental outcomes, but also how context interacts and sometimes even shapes the biological system (Gottlieb 2007; O'Donnell and Meaney 2020; Zhang and Meaney 2010). Such new insights into the interplay and transactions between biology, behavior and context need to be taken into account when developing concrete implications for entrepreneurial education.

6.3   IMPLICATIONS FOR POLICY

A deeper and evidence-based understanding of regional macro-psychological differences relevant for entrepreneurship is, of course, highly relevant for public policy (Audretsch et al. 2007, 2019). Designing effective initiatives for the development of a local entrepreneurial culture has become a major policy target around the globe (OECD 2020) but it is somewhat unclear what an entrepreneurial culture actually is, and how one can measure and develop it. The geography of entrepreneurial psychology offers one concrete way of conceptualizing such an entrepreneurial culture. One main implication for policy is therefore that there is reason to account for regional differences of people's personality characteristics and mentalities, as well as associated regional dynamics. Hence, a one-size-fits-all policy approach that could be appropriate for all regions may not exist. Political strategies that work well in regions that have a more entrepreneurial macro-psychological profile and vivid start-up activities could be ineffective in regions where self-employment is uncommon and not regarded a serious option among the population.

Regional entrepreneurship policy should, therefore, not only consider and target the formal regulations and regional conditions that are relevant for starting and running a business, but also take soft factors into account like the local psychological make-up (Stuetzer et al. 2018). Lowering hurdles and paving the way for new businesses may not work well if there is hardly anyone willing to be self-employed. Each region might have its own specific macro-psychological profile and regional policies should try to build on, and leverage, local strengths (and compensate for/reduce less conducive factors).

In regions that already have a pronounced culture of entrepreneurship, policy should be careful to preserve this culture and open avenues to overcome development bottlenecks. Regions where a culture of entrepreneurship is lacking may require considerably more attention and effort to build such a culture. As a first step, such a policy approach should try to identify the reasons for the relatively low levels of regional entrepreneurship. The results of such an analysis can then serve as a basis for the development of a region-specific strategy to improve the level of entrepreneurial activity. The finding of many empirical studies that regional levels of entrepreneurship are persistent over rather long periods of time (the important persistence phenomenon; Fritsch and Mueller 2007; Fritsch and Wyrwich 2017a; see also Chapter 4) suggests that policies which aim at stimulating an entrepreneurial culture may require long periods of time before significant changes can be noticed. Clearly, existing research in the geography of entrepreneurial psychology suggests that creating an entrepreneurship culture is a long-term strategy. However, once such a culture is created it may work as a regional capital stock that generates long-lasting positive effects on entrepreneurial thinking and acting in the region.

One may, however, pose a question about the legitimacy of a policy that attempts to brainwash a regional population by creating a culture of entrepreneurship – a form of social engineering that uses human psychology to generate certain behaviors. This ethical question involves at least two main aspects. First, is creating a more entrepreneurial culture indeed an appropriate policy goal (OECD 2020)? Second, do the instruments leave sufficient freedom to persons who want to escape such a policy? The first question concerns the justification of strengthening certain aspects of a regional culture. Entrepreneurship is not a goal in itself but is commonly regarded as a means to achieve more economic welfare, i.e., promote economic growth and make the economy more resilient to external shocks. In a regional context, fostering entrepreneurship can be a particular strategy to help lagging regions improve their economic performance and to catch up. Stimulating entrepreneurial behavior is, for example, a key element of the European Union's strategy of smart specialization (McCann and Ortega-Argilés 2016). Hence, the first question concerns the general legitimacy of regional growth policy that is, however, largely undisputed in most developed countries. However, if changing the local culture is indeed a long-term endeavor, polices aiming to boost local entrepreneurship relatively quickly might need to build on the local, existing culture (instead of quickly changing it in a significant way). This means accepting and building on the existing local profile that not only includes the economic profile but also the macro-psychological profile.

The second question pertains to the instruments that are applied for creating or strengthening a regional culture of entrepreneurship. Real-world examples for measures that are consciously aimed at promoting an entrepreneurial culture, such as support in developing entrepreneurial abilities through entrepreneurship education, assistance for potential entre-preneurs and fostering knowledge transfer and stimulating peer effects, do not restrict individual behavior but may, of course, be opposed for ideological reasons. Thus, we do not call for mass interventions changing personality structures of whole regions, as this would be unethical. According to the literature in geographical psychology (e.g., Rentfrow et al. 2008), another mechanism for local culture change would be selective migration in a way to attract entrepreneurially minded people and set economic incentives, discouraging out-migration of such people. However, this might be, again, a rather long-term endeavor and again there may be some ethical questions to be considered.

Besides the questions of whether and how public policy should attempt to change the local culture by addressing the region's underlying macro-psychology, *mapping* of existing local macro-psychological profiles could provide policymak-ers with important information that they can use for designing and targeting political schemes and programs (see Guzman and Stern 2015).

7. Agenda for future research

7.1 ADVANCES IN MACRO-PSYCHOLOGICAL THEORY

Future research in the geography of entrepreneurship psychology should put a particular emphasis on making significant advances in theory building and development. Theories are an important pillar of the research field, they "reflect, in highly abstract terms, the organization of a discipline's knowledge base" (Suddaby 2014, p. 407). Investing pragmatically *in the process* of theory building is challenging (Weick 1995) but should be highly valued and recognized in the field. As described in Shepherd and Suddaby (2017), such theory-building efforts can be guided by the literature on the process of theory building itself. Tools and approaches to theorizing can include, for example, engaged scholarship (Van de Ven and Johnson 2006), metaphor (Cornelissen 2005), case studies (Eisenhardt and Graebner 2007) and balancing novelty and continuity (Locke and Golden-Biddle 1997). Continuous effective transactions between theory building and theory testing are essential to develop, refine or revise theories (Lévesque et al. 2020).

However, theory building and development also comes with certain dangers for the scientific progress in the field (Suddaby 2014). Groups of theories, or paradigms, can build closed pockets in a field that maintain certain dynamics in the scientific process that might be useful for individual researchers or groups of researchers championing these theories, but could also hamper ultimate progress in the field overall (e.g., via ingroup–outgroup dynamics such as ingroup bias and favoritism; Efferson et al. 2008). It is important to keep in mind that "theory has the potential to balkanize the community" because it can be "an effective barrier to the movement of knowledge across subgroups" of theories within a field (Suddaby 2014, p. 409). Such negative dynamics can be particularly pronounced in the case of paradigms. Suddaby (2014, p. 409) states that "paradigm wars are a blood sport draining resources and energy and reducing communication, ultimately failing to advance any of the values of theory".

Therefore, if there are different paradigms and thus (competing) research perspectives and groups of theories in the field, it seems advisable to (a) clearly articulate the existence of paradigms, their differences and overlap, as well as the implications for research and practice; (b) avoid closed pockets and echo chambers in the scientific discourse to minimize a danger of balkanization of the community by fostering the flow of knowledge between subgroups of theories in the field; and (c) if possible attempt to conceptually connect and integrate paradigms and research perspectives. Translated into future theorizing on the geography of entrepreneurial psychology, this could mean a number of implications.

Scholars should invest more effort in connecting and integrating leading paradigms figuring prominently in the micro-level psychology of entrepreneurship – not only to foster communication and effective transactions between subgroups of theories and research perspectives, but also to contribute to the important goal of academic distinctiveness and uniqueness of entrepreneurship research, compared to the mere application of single theories and paradigms from other fields (Venkataraman 2019). Psychology is a very diverse field with very different paradigms, research perspectives and foci – a prime example of what Suddaby (2014) describes as a challenging diversity of paradigms and subgroups of theories in a specific field.

In this book we have tried to simplify the conceptual structure of the contemporary micro-level psychology of entrepreneurship by distinguishing two major paradigms that have, in recent years, figured particularly prominently in empirical entrepreneurship research concerned with psychological topics. First, is the action-oriented paradigm, which puts entrepreneurial actions and how single actions are psychologically regulated in the center of conceptual and empirical approaches to the psychology of entrepreneurship (Frese 2009; Frese and Gielnik 2014). Second, is the person-oriented paradigm, which starts with the individual and focuses on the individuality and the personality of a person and how this shapes his or her entrepreneurial outcomes (Kerr et al. 2018; Krueger et al. 2000; McClelland 1961; Schumpeter 1934; Shane et al. 2010). This comparison, with respect to both differences and overlap between these two paradigms, is therefore comparable to the classic "who vs. what" debate that has been occupying the field of entrepreneur-focused research for more than three decades (Gartner 1988; Ramoglou et al. 2020; Rauch and Frese 2007; see also Landström 2020).

Future theorizing could attempt to connect and integrate both paradigms if possible. Such efforts could address questions such as how the psychological regulation of entrepreneurial actions (the core in action regulation theory) interacts with macro-psychological factors and mechanism. Is an effective action regulation at the individual level a mediator between context and entrepreneur? This in turn could operate in the context→individual direction where a macro-psychological regional profile conducive to entrepreneurship facilitates the individual-level cognitive cycle of prototypical entrepreneurial action sequences in this region (cycles comprised of (1) goals/redefinition of tasks; (2) information collection and prognosis; (3) plan and execution; and (4) monitoring and feedback; see Frese 2009). This could help explain why regions with a more entrepreneurial macro-psychological profile tend to be more successful in entrepreneurship and economic growth (e.g., Garretsen et al. 2018; Obschonka et al. 2016; Stuetzer et al. 2018). The psychological action regulation in local entrepreneurs in these regions may occur in a more effective and persistent way because, for instance, a positive entrepreneurial climate could facilitate personal initiative, and the single components of the cognitive action cycle in local entrepreneurs.

The mediating effect of action regulation at the individual level could also operate in the opposite direction (individual→context), where individual-level action regulation constitutes the macro-psychological entrepreneurial profile of a region. Since the geography of entrepreneurship psychology typically starts from micro-level psychological concepts and theories and adopts them at the macro-level to map macro-psychological factors, one could also ask whether a limited expansion of such programs to specific groups might be able to indirectly alter the macro-psychology of that region towards a more entrepreneurial climate. Note that we do not call for unethical mass intervention programs to change the personality of a whole regional populace, but for a limited used of action-regulation training that targets barriers to entrepreneurship. If more people in a region act in an entrepreneurial manner, this in turn could indirectly stimulate local entrepreneurial thinking and action. Such questions applying a macro-psychological lens to action regulation can contribute to our knowledge of the geography of psychological agency, which is interested in the agentic capacities of regions (Huggins and Thompson 2019).

Finally, future theorizing that integrates action-oriented and person-oriented paradigms could also elaborate our knowledge of historical processes. For example, it could help explain why old industrial centers, where large-scale industries dominated whole generations of people and local culture for a long time, might show a less entrepreneurial macro-psychological profile and lower entrepreneurship rates compared to other regions (Glaeser et al. 2015; Stuetzer et al.

2016). The industrial heritage may have left a deep psychological imprint that, until today, affects action regulation mechanisms in local populations (Obschonka 2018). If this is really true, then action regulation training could be a particularly promising tool to boost entrepreneurship in such old industrial regions that have witnessed strong industrial decline in recent decades, associated with systematic macro-psychological patterns (Abdellaoui et al. 2019; Obschonka et al. 2018). Selectively targeted intervention programs for key groups that already possess many entrepreneurship relevant characteristics but are held back from entrepreneurial action by living in a region with a non-entrepreneurial climate might receive a decisive nudge through action regulation programs, such as, for example, teaching personal initiative programs (e.g., Campos et al. 2017).

While we have focused on action-oriented and person-oriented paradigms, another major paradigm relevant for future theorizing in the field is, of course, the culture-oriented paradigm (e.g., cross-cultural psychology that focuses on connections between psychological phenomena and cultural symbols, practices and norms (Berry et al. 1992; Kashima 2016; Kashima et al. 2019; Keller and Greenfield 2000; Oishi and Graham 2010)). Scholars have already started to integrate approaches from cross-cultural psychology into a person-oriented personality approach to better understand the geography of entrepreneurial psychology (Huggins et al. 2018; Huggins and Thompson 2019).

7.2   BRIDGING ACADEMIC DISCIPLINES

Besides an integration of different paradigms stemming from the individual-level psychology of entrepreneurship, future theorizing on the geography of entrepreneurial psychology should also continue to apply an interdisciplinary perspective – bridging disciplines such as psychology, geography, sociology, history and management. Given the pronounced differences of theoretical approaches among these disciplines it is hardly expected that they could be integrated under a common roof. The differences in approaches and particularly in empirical results that are found when looking through a diverse disciplinary lens constitute challenges for further theoretical developments.

One such type of bridge to the economics discipline is behavioral economics, a field where researchers have, for a number of decades, attempted to develop a more realistic vision of the individual than the simple model of *Homo economicus*, a rational and utility-maximizing human being that is at the heart of economic theorizing (Cartwright 2018). This research investigates the determinants of factual individual behavior and decision-making that are key topics of psychology, mainly on an empirical basis.

Individual decisions are always made in a certain context that often has significant effects on these decisions (Welter 2011; Welter and Baker 2020). Hence, another discipline where ties can be established is economic geography. Research should systematically consider the main dimensions of the context such as industry and region. It would, for example, be interesting to learn more about how location and accessibility, industry structure, agglomeration and level of economic development shape personalities, preferences and behaviors. There is clearly an important overlap between the academic disciplines of geography and psychology in these respects. Accounting for the psychology and culture of a place could be a promising avenue of research for both disciplines, as well as for sociology which deals with diverse aspects of the societal conditions. The recognition that the psychology and culture of places can have pronounced historical roots indicates the relevance of historical research. How do experiences of a population, such as wartime destruction, economic crises or long periods subjected to suppressive regimes, shape the psychology of a regional population? How does a collective memory of such developments influence individual behavior?

Besides the geography-inspired research into historical roots of contemporary regional differences in macro-psychological characteristics, economic geography also offers research avenues to the processes of how macro-psychological characteristics affect individual behavior in context. Among the research paradigms in economic geography, the relational approach promises a link to the geography of entrepreneurial psychology. Most importantly, relational economic geography puts the economic actors, such as individuals and firms, at the center of the analysis. It is the relations between those actors that shape innovation, learning and production processes, among other things, within a regional space (Bathelt and Glückler 2003). The input of geography of entrepreneurial psychology lies in influencing relations between the human actors. As discussed in Chapter 3.3, individual personality characteristics shape the mental models of individuals and at a more aggregate level the shared mental model of individuals within a region. It can thereby influence information processing and decision-making.

Let us look, for example, at the Big Five trait openness. At the individual level this trait involves curiosity, preference for variety, thin mental boundaries and imagination. It is thus of little surprise that openness is associated with creativity, knowledge creation and entrepreneurial activity with modest correlations (McCrae 1996). The importance for economic effects at a regional level stems from a multiplier effect as individual openness affects many daily interrelations over years (Funder and Ozer 2019). This becomes magnified in that there is a cluster of interacting people scoring high in openness. Those people will engage in repeated discussions, challenge each other's views and will obtain more creative results in brainstorming sessions repeatedly over time. Thus, although the individual correlations of openness with creativity, innovation and entrepreneurial activity are relatively modest, its cumulative effect in a network of relationships at a regional level can have a stronger impact in the long run. A research program using the lens of relational economic geography could look at the influence of personality characteristics in knowledge creation and interactions in regional networks.

Finally, research on the industry context, which is a particular focus of industrial sociology and industrial economics, should be further integrated with macro-psychological approaches. While industrial economics deals mainly with market structure and competition within industries, research in industrial sociology focuses on work conditions and industrial relationships in different industries. Both economics and sociology make important contributions to labor market research.

7.3   RESEARCH: POLICY INTERACTION

One major task for the next generation of research on the geography of entrepreneurial psychology is to take stock of the growing body of theoretical and empirical insights in this field to elaborate on concrete implications and concepts for policy and practice, as well as, equally important, to perform research on the effects of policies and practices. A particularly important research focus should be on public policy, for example public policy aiming at entrepreneurial eco-systems or, more broadly, regional differences in entrepreneurial thinking and acting. This includes grassroots or everyday entrepreneurship where new firms that stay small and are not based on innovations (Welter et al. 2017) but also high-impact entrepreneurship characterized by growing and innovative firms.

Geographical research on psychological factors and mechanisms behind entrepreneurship also comes with broader implications for adjacent policy fields such as those that primarily target innovation, employment, migration or regional development, given that entrepreneurship makes such a broad promise to society by driving innovations, creating jobs and generating economic growth. These policy topics have a strong geographic component that often requires consideration of "soft" regional factors. The geography of entrepreneurial psychology can offer new ways of thinking about, and measuring, such soft factors, based on established micro-level psychological concepts and insights. It can also offer models that describe the regional mechanisms why such soft regional factors exist, how they persist or not, and how they actually shape entrepreneurial thinking and acting as well as individual-level psychological mechanisms.

One of the key issues for public policy *and* research will be to address the question whether entrepreneurship policies should attempt *to change* local macro-psychological profiles (e.g., entrepreneurial personality) or whether such policies should simply *accept* existing regional differences in personality traits (Rentfrow et al. 2008) and design effective policies that are specifically tailored to the existing local psychological profile. Arguably, a time perspective should play a prominent role in these considerations, e.g., long-term policies could target deeper macro-psychological change processes whereas short-term policies could design and implement schemes and programs that are tailored to the current psychological profile. For example, if old coal regions show, on average, a less entrepreneurial personality profile than non-coal regions, short-term policies addressing economic development and structural change in old coal regions could attempt to directly compensate for these less entrepreneurial basic personality tendencies in the region. Such policies could, for example, compensate for less strong entrepreneurial psychological agency in the region i.e., by introducing stronger incentives or other strong motivators of entrepreneurial thinking and acting.

Another approach for policy can be to target the self-reinforcing effects of entrepreneurial mindsets and entrepreneurial actions in regions that can have either a virtuous or a vicious spin (see Chapters 3 and 5). The presence of (successful) entrepreneurial role models could help in initiating an entrepreneurial culture, which in turn may affect the psychological make-up of a region and make it more likely that other people become entrepreneurs. A supportive policy and the emergence of an entrepreneurial culture can also attract migrants with entrepreneurial mindsets. The Munich University of Technology is an example of such a deliberate pro-entrepreneurship policy, which includes several entrepreneurship scholars, entrepreneurship education programs, a network of support agencies and brokering contacts to business angels and venture capitalists.

Such regional policies should, however, take psychological research insights on the detrimental effects of poor behavior seriously (e.g., research on extrinsic vs. intrinsic motivation, research on cognitive dissonance or research on self-concept factors, like life narratives and identity). Another approach with respect to short-term policies in old coal regions is to identify the unique macro-psychological strengths of the region and then try to build policies that leverage these soft factors as a unique psychological capital of the region. Research could assist in defining and exploring such potential strengths.

A particularly interesting approach could be the study of macro-psychological factors related to social capital (e.g., solidarity in the region, social networks, weak and strong ties) that might be conducive to entrepreneurship (Davidsson and Honig 2003; Kim and Aldrich 2005). Such a focus on macro-psychological strengths of a certain region would be similar to smart specialization policies where regions identify their current economic strengths and invest in activities that build on and leverage these strengths (Grillitsch 2016; McCann and Ortega-Argilés 2016). Research could help in developing and evaluating such policy schemes and programs.

Research should not only be targeted towards short-term policies but also long-term policies, particularly since we know from research that history, and thus a longer time frame, plays an important role for the geography of entrepreneurial psychology. For example, research could study the slow, gradual change in a regional personality profile (e.g., in old coal regions).

As discussed in Obschonka (2018), policies and the wider public should also acknowledge and recognize regional psychological profiles and idiosyncrasies as they exist – they reflect human beings and their collective private characteristics and, as shown by research, they are also reflective of the historical industrial imprint of the region and thus also of the biographies and achievements of many generations in these regions. Moreover, policies and research alike should carefully follow ethical principles recommended for such people-focused projects (e.g., American Psychological Association 2017). Such principles, for example, advise against the use of certain psychological labels for people and whole groups of people (e.g., labels with a negative connotation).

7.4   PSYCHOLOGICAL DIVERSITY OF PLACES

Human diversity is one of the most important research topics of our modern times (Gelfand 2019). So far, macro-psychological entrepreneurship research has mainly focused on regional levels in personality traits and profiles but future research could also study the *within-region diversity* in traits and profiles – how different/diverse people are in the same region from each other in terms of their traits and profiles, which may determine macro-psychological diversity in the region. There are compelling theoretical arguments that speak for such a research focus on psychological diversity within regions. For example, in her seminal theorizing, Jane Jacobs (1961, 1969), one of the pioneers in the field of urban planning and what makes cities entrepreneurial and innovative (Beaudry and Schiffauerova 2009; de Groot et al. 2016), put people and their city life in the center of her thinking, with the key assertion that urban density and particularly diversity of people are conducive to creativity. This hypothesis has been largely confirmed empirically, mainly by focusing on the diversity of industries within cities and regions (e.g., Glaeser et al. 1992; see also Karlsson et al. 2021).

Future research could address Jane Jacobs' people-focus to regional economic activity and wealth more directly by studying the question whether psychological diversity in people also stimulates entrepreneurship and innovation. The study of diversity in people within regions has gained some attention in economic research over recent years (Ashraf and Galor 2013; Florida 2004, 2010; Nathan 2015; Nathan and Lee 2013). Geographical psychology research (Rentfrow 2020) can inform the economics of diversity (Nathan 2015) and vice versa.

7.5   DISENTANGLING THE PURELY REGIONAL FROM INDIVIDUAL-LEVEL EFFECTS

Region-level correlations between psychological factors and entrepreneurship can reflect a variety of mechanisms that operate at the regional and/or individual level. For example, if a region has a greater stock of people with an entrepreneurial personality profile it may show higher entrepreneurship rates because there are more entrepreneurially minded people that start their own business and are self-employed. This would be an individual-level mechanism (entrepreneurial personality correlates with entrepreneurial behavior), studied at the regional level. At the same time, it could also be that the relatively many people with an entrepreneurial personality profile in a region establish and maintain certain entrepreneurial norms and attitudes (Marshall 1920), create peer and demonstration effects by running their own businesses or that there exist (other) informal and formal institutions conducive to entrepreneurship. Such increased entrepreneurial conditions in a regional context (see Figure 4.1) may then affect entrepreneurial motivation and behavior also in people with low entrepreneurial personality profiles. Hence, high levels of self-employment in such a region could result from pure individual-level mechanisms or from the interplay of individual characteristics within the regional context.

It would be interesting to disentangle these different types of effects in order to assess their relative strength. This could be done by means of multi-level analysis that includes data at the individual level (e.g., psychological factors and entrepreneurial behavior) and corresponding data at the region level. Based on such an approach one could test whether individual-level entrepreneurial behavior is better predictable by individual-level psychological factors or by corresponding psychological factors at the regional macro-level. How strong is the purely regional effect, above and beyond the individual-level effect? Future studies should particularly try to shed more light on the actual nature of the regional mechanisms linking the geography of entrepreneurial psychology to entrepreneurial behavior and success which is still an under-researched area. It would go back to very seminal thinking about the role of regions and places for economic development (Marshall 1920; Saxenian 1996) – something that certain places have in their psychological structure that stimulates and enables processes leading to better economic outcomes.

Such future research should also attempt to study smaller spatial units – such as city centers, city districts, or even the street level (Guzman and Stern 2015). Many regional mechanisms linking psychology and entrepreneurship might operate at relatively fine-grained spatial levels and it is important to catch such mechanisms, and the inter-regional variation in such mechanisms and effects, by zooming in on smaller spatial units.

7.6   STABILITY AND CHANGE OVER TIME

Future research should also invest more effort in applying a time perspective – how does the geography of entrepreneurial psychology change over time? Whereas the first generation of research in this field was mostly concerned with mapping psychological factors relevant for entrepreneurship, the next generation should look at it by applying a dynamic framework and considering the time axis in more detail. How do regional psychological and entrepreneurial outcomes co-evolve and co-develop over time (Stuetzer et al. 2016)? What is chicken, what is egg? Did entrepreneurial psychological factors of regions emerge first, and are regional entrepreneurial outcomes purely a consequence of this psychological map? Or was it the other way around?

Research could try to use experiments to answer these questions. For example, if a specific region introduced a certain extremely entrepreneurship-friendly public policy that increases local entrepreneurship rates. Does this also result in an increase of local entrepreneurial psychological factors over time (which cannot be explained otherwise)? Another idea is to look at major, unpredicted economic crises that suppress entrepreneurial activity. Such studies could examine regional psychology→entrepreneurial outcomes effect by examining whether regional psychological profiles, measured before a crisis, predict entrepreneurial outcomes (including economic resilience) during a crisis (Obschonka et al. 2016). Studies could examine the entrepreneurial outcomes→regional psychology effect by analyzing change in regional psychological factors during and after a crisis as a function of a decline in entrepreneurial activity/success associated with the crisis. However, a working hypothesis should be that regional differences in entrepreneurial psychology should show substantial degrees of stability over time. This view is supported by research examining the stability of region-level personality traits (Elleman et al. 2018) and by historical research linking present-day regional personality difference to major historical epochs and events (which also implies considerable stability since these epochs and events have left a deep macro-psychological imprint) (Fritsch et al. 2020c; Obschonka et al. 2018; Talhelm et al. 2014).

It might also be interesting to study how the current digital revolution in society may shape the psychological landscape of regions and nations. If past research indicates that such major industrial and technological revolutions might have left a deep psychological imprint on regions (Obschonka 2018), the ongoing second machine age that is driven by data and artificial intelligence (AI) and not by coal and steam engines as in the first machine age (Brynjolfsson and McAfee 2014) might have the potential for similarly deep psychological effects that can last for a longer period. Future research should also intensify efforts for a better understanding of how regional and local *physical* factors of the environment (e.g., landscape, climate, air quality) shape and maintain geographical variation in entrepreneurial psychology (Götz et al. 2020; Lu 2020; Oishi 2014; Talhelm et al. 2014; Wei et al. 2017).

When studying concrete patterns of change in geographical psychology associated with entrepreneurship, researchers could apply research perspectives from individual-level personality psychology, which has developed elaborate concepts, techniques and methods to estimate both stability and change in personality. This could, for example, include mean-level and rank-order stability and change of personality over the life-span (Caspi and Roberts 2001; Roberts and DelVecchio 2000), typologies of events and conditions under which change is particularly likely (Bleidorn et al. 2018; Specht et al. 2011, 2014), and typologies of change patterns such as pliable processes, elastic processes and short-term fluctuations (Roberts 2018). Do regions show similar change patterns as individuals do in terms of region-level psychological factors?

7.7   MIGRATION

Another highly important topic for future research deals with various aspects of migration. The psychology of regions and places is closely linked to selective migration patterns (Rentfrow et al. 2008). We know that personality traits shape migration decisions (e.g., Campbell 2019; Fouarge et al. 2019; Jokela 2009, 2014) and whole regions show systematic macro-psychological outflux and influx patterns (Abdellaoui et al. 2019; Obschonka et al. 2018). It is highly likely that selective migration plays a key role in the emergence and persistence of a geography of entrepreneurial psychology which might be even more important than local social influences in shaping local personality profiles (Jokela 2020).

Empirical studies of such patterns are complex and require comprehensive data. Ideally, such future macro-psychological research would have access to large datasets that include information on migrants' region of origin and region of destination in order to map macro-psychological migration streams between regions. Moreover, it would be desirable to be able to identify the main reasons for moving from one place to another. In what way do psychological constellations play a role here as compared to, for instance, purely economic reasons? What are the push and pull factors? What places attract what kinds of people? What kinds of people leave certain places?

Another interesting question concerns the potential effect of the migration experience itself on the migrant and collectively on regions populated by migrants (Lönnqvist et al. 2011). In what way does migration in general and selective migration of people with a certain mindset change the macro-psychological profile of a region? The entrepreneurship literature deems migrants as a particularly interesting research subject due to the entrepreneurial agency they often demonstrate (Baycan-Levent and Nijkamp 2009; Kloosterman 2010). Do arriving migrants and their offspring bring a more entrepreneurial psychological climate to a region? And if migration as such requires migrants to adopt an open mindset in the acculturation process, do also whole regions that experience large amounts of in-migration become more open minded?

Such migration research has also the potential to address the selection vs. socialization question in geographical psychology (Rentfrow et al. 2008): Do regions 1) become more entrepreneurial because more entrepreneurially minded people move there as they are attracted by an opportunity, local role models and entrepreneurial peers, institutions conducive to entrepreneurship; or 2) do more entrepreneurial regions make people living and working in these regions more entrepreneurial over time? How can it be explained that the incoming population in regions that experienced a more or less complete exchange of the local population after World War II has to a considerable degree adjusted to the long-term entrepreneurial tradition or culture of their destination (e.g., Fritsch et al. 2019; Fritsch, Pylak and Wyrwich 2019)?[1]

Finally, research on the role of migration for the geography of entrepreneurial psychology could also consider forced migration such as large refugee waves (Obschonka, Hahn and Bajwa 2018; Shepherd et al. 2020).

---

[1]   A further example are a number of small villages in rural Germany that after World War II experienced huge inflows of expellees from former German territories that partly adjusted to the entrepreneurial culture of these regions but also induced changes (Braun and Kvasnicka 2014; Fritsch and Wyrwich 2017a; Semrad 2015). It is particularly remarkable in these cases that the immigrants were not allowed to choose their region of destination but were allocated to regions by the public administration.

7.8   TRADITION AND COLLECTIVE MEMORY OF PLACES

Places and regions can have distinct psychological representations of traditions that are rooted in their history. These cultures and traditions that are associated with the aggregate psychological traits (Freytag and Thurik 2007, p. 123) in the regional population are supposed to be an important source of long-term persistence of regional entrepreneurial activity, even if a region experiences disruptive changes to its social, economic and political conditions (see Chapter 4). Examples of regions where entrepreneurship persisted despite a more or less complete exchange of the population (Chapter 4.3) strongly indicate that such cultures and traditions can include more than just an intergenerational transmission of personality traits but also an identity or collective memory that is independent of its current population.

This collective memory that distinguishes a certain place or region from others is a social construct that provides places with a stable identity and meaning – e.g., "where it all began" or "the place to be". The collective memory can become manifest in material remains such as buildings, traditions, common narratives and images (Jones et al. 2019; Olick et al. 2011). Memory as a collective psychological mechanism (Hirst et al. 2018; Roediger and DeSoto 2014) can have considerable effects on the collective behavior of individuals as well as on organizations and public policy. Although such effects have been recognized for a long time – Alfred Marshall's (1920) notion of something being "in the air" is a prominent example – the phenomenon is still not well understood in economic research.

Generally, little is known about the emergence of a positive attitude towards entrepreneurship in a region that may be relatively stable over time. One factor that is supposed to contribute to such an attitude is demonstration and peer effects generated by the entrepreneurial activities in a region, but there are probably also other mechanisms that are currently unexplored. With regard to demonstration and peer effects, it is unclear what types of entrepreneurship have a relatively strong impact, what types are more or less negligible and if there is entrepreneurial activity that impacts the regional entrepreneurial attitude in a negative way. It is plausible to assume that successful new and young firms in the region may create strong incentives to also choose self-employment as an occupation, but it also appears plausible to assume that failure of start-ups has the opposite effect.

7.9 THE RATIONALITY AND NON-RATIONALITY OF REGIONS

Economic research informed by psychological perspectives has delivered important insights into the rationality *and* non-rationality of human decision-making (Camerer and Loewenstein 2003; Kahneman 2003; Tversky and Kahneman 1974). One particularly interesting focus in this research deals with the bounds of rationality of economic agents and cognitive biases (Gigerenzer and Selten 2002; Simon 1991). New research on the geography of entrepreneurial psychology could address the question to what extent not only individuals but also whole regional populations behave non-rationally and how this then can inform practice and policymaking. Can, for example, regional differences in entrepreneurial personality traits and their effects on entrepreneurial outcomes as demonstrated in previous studies be interpreted as non-rationality of regions – as something that classical economic theory would not incorporate? For example, if regions react differently to (unforeseeable) macro-economic crises like the global financial crisis (GFC) or the COVID-19 pandemic, and this can be in part explained by regional personality differences (e.g., Garretsen et al. 2020; Obschonka et al. 2016), then this effect would be something that classic economic theories are not able to explain; it would demonstrate the non-rationality of regions and the economic decision-making and behavior of local populations. It would thus show that we also need to take into account, and better understand, the drivers of this non-rationality.

Micro-level psychological science (e.g., Baumeister 2003) as well as geographical psychology can deliver important insights in this regard – how to conceptualize, measure and interpret non-rational behavior in the context of entrepreneurship. Research could, of course, also study how the psychological environment influences decision-making by entrepreneurs via micro–macro interactions (see Gigerenzer 2004). In other words, one so far understudied yet potentially important context factor for individual-level entrepreneurial decision-making could be geographical psychological factors (e.g., the local entrepreneurial climate, norms and attitudes). Do entrepreneurs/start-ups make less rational decisions and are they more prone to cognitive biases in a region or place with a particularly entrepreneurial psychological makeup (e.g., higher collective levels in an entrepreneurial personality profile) compared to entrepreneurs/start-ups in other regions/ places? By applying a context-minded perspective, such research would also contribute to the important literature on the prevalence and role of cognitive bias in entrepreneurs (Busenitz and Barney 1997; Koellinger et al. 2007; Lowe and Ziedonis 2006).

Taken together, research into the geography of entrepreneurial psychology has great potential to enrich our knowledge of the (non-)rationality of regions (and of single entrepreneurs) and future research should direct attention towards these fundamental questions of rationality at the regional level.

7.10 MICRO–MACRO FIT: THE GEOGRAPHY OF ENTREPRENEURIAL PSYCHOLOGY AS A MODERATOR IN ENTREPRENEURSHIP RESEARCH

Taking context seriously and examining how context shapes mechanisms in entrepreneurship has become a major research focus in contemporary entrepreneurship research (Welter and Gartner 2016). From this perspective, the geography of entrepreneurial psychology can also be understood as a context factor for entrepreneurship. For example, with the availability of geographical macro-psychological data also come more opportunities to study micro–macro interactions in entrepreneurship, besides cognitive biases as described above. To illustrate, inspired by person–city/region fit, research in personality psychology (e.g., Bleidorn et al. 2016; Jokela et al. 2015), Zhou et al. (2019) analyzed personality data from around 26,000 Chinese residents across 42 major Chinese cities, including around 1,000 Chinese entrepreneurs. Predicting individual-level indicators of entrepreneurial success of these entrepreneurs, multi-level polynomial regression and response surface plots revealed that, besides the effect of individual-level traits and city-level traits, it was particularly the interaction between individual-level traits and city-level traits that shed new light on potential success mechanisms. For example, for the case of agreeableness, the results showed that entrepreneurs who score *high* on agreeableness tend to be somewhat unsuccessful if they conduct their business in a city with a *low* agreeableness level. In contrast, entrepreneurs scoring *low* on agreeableness and conduct their business in a city with a *high* agreeableness level tend to be relatively successful.

Combining information on geographical macro-psychological characteristics with micro-data opens up an exciting whole new research agenda studying the geography of entrepreneurial psychology as a moderator in the micro-level investigation of entrepreneurial behavior and success. Future research should address the fundamental question to what extent micro-level relationships in entrepreneurship are universal or actually conditional of such macro-psychological context factors. Could, for example, a certain entrepreneurial trait be very adaptive in terms of increasing the likelihood for entrepreneurial success in a certain macro-psychological environment, whereas in other macro-psychological environments the same trait is maladaptive? For example, one explanation for the person–city interaction on the context-specific effect of agreeableness on entrepreneurial success in the study by Zhou et al. (2019) could be a fish-in-a-shark-tank mechanism: those entrepreneurs that are high in agreeableness and operate their business in a city scoring low in agreeableness might be less successful because of the unfavorable constellation and micro–macro dynamics between being an agreeable entrepreneur who therefore may focus on harmony and cooperation in social interactions and the highly competitive, aggressive psychological business environments of a shark tank city with many people scoring low in agreeableness.

Such research on micro–macro fit effects and dynamics should not only involve context moderation of psychological effects and mechanisms, but could also enrich other types of entrepreneurship research such as (1) strategy: e.g., are certain entrepreneurial strategies more adaptive in certain macro-psychological environments than in others?; (2) human and social capital: What type of human and social capital is needed in specific macro-psychological environments?; (3) entrepreneurial finance: How does the macro-psychological environment affect the allocation of financial resources for entrepreneurs or how optimistic and risky do venture capitalists invest in entrepreneurs as a function of the local macro-psychological climate?; or (4) innovation and technology: Are innovations produced and adopted more effectively in certain macro-psychological environments than in others?

In other words, the emerging field of the geography of entrepreneurial psychology could help the field of entrepreneurship research and practice to obtain a more complete picture on the relationship between context-driven relevant dynamics and mechanisms in entrepreneurship (Welter 2011; Welter and Baker 2020; Welter and Gartner 2016).

7.11   IMPLICATIONS FOR SUBJECTIVE AND PSYCHOLOGICAL WELL-BEING AND MENTAL HEALTH

Entrepreneurship requires certain levels of personal well-being in entrepreneurs but often also comes with implications for their well-being such as that it can affect hedonic and eudaemonic well-being in various ways. This is the story told in many studies on the subjective and psychological well-being, stress and mental health in the micro-level psychology of entrepreneurship (Ryff 2019; Stephan 2018; Stephan et al. 2020; Wiklund, Nikolaev et al. 2019; Wiklund et al. 2020; Wincent and Örtqvist 2009). But how can the geography of entrepreneurial psychology inform this important research and practice field?

First, the geography of entrepreneurial psychology could be again studied as a moderator. Do psychological processes shaping personal well-being, stress and mental health in entrepreneurs differ or interact with the macro-psychological environment? Revising the example from Zhou et al. (2019) again, are entrepreneurs with a particularly unfavorable person–city personality fit more prone to entrepreneurial stress and burnout? In psychological science we currently see a growing literature testing and documenting well-being benefits of psychological person–region fit (Bleidorn et al. 2016; Ebert et al. 2020; Götz et al. 2018; Jokela et al. 2015). This literature could inform future entrepreneurship research interested in the relationship between personal well-being, on the one hand, and the psychological dynamics associated with micro–macro interactions, on the other. It is well known that well-being processes are often context-sensitive and this should not be different in entrepreneurs.

Second, future research could examine whether the macro-psychological environment also has more direct effects on the personal well-being of entrepreneurs. For example, it seems plausible to ask whether a certain macro-psychological environment that is particularly entrepreneurial (e.g., higher regional levels in an entrepreneurial personality profile) represents some kind of psychological resource in the stress process in local entrepreneurs, maybe via a psychological climate of entrepreneurial optimism that is focused on gains/opportunities instead of on (potential) losses. Such gains and conservation of resources is deemed to be an important ingredient in the stress process (Hobfoll 1989; see also Hobfoll 2001). Another channel through which a particularly entrepreneurial macro-psychological environment could impact personal well-being is social support. We know that social support is one of the important protective factors in stress and well-being processes (Cohen and Wills 1985; Vinokur and Caplan 1987), and that social support mechanisms are also shaped by the wider psychological local context (Taylor et al. 2004). A local psychological climate that is positive in terms of entrepreneurial attitudes, role models and norms could stimulate more social support for local entrepreneurs, support that may not only be needed in stressful and challenging situations and longer periods of uncertainty and hardship for entrepreneurs (Klyver et al. 2018), but of course also to cope with more extreme situations such as entrepreneurial failure (Shepherd 2003, 2004; Shepherd et al. 2009).

Finally, future research could determine at what spatial level (ranging from small-city districts over regions to countries) well-being implications of the geography of entrepreneurial psychology are strong. One working hypothesis could be that the more proximal and relevant to the individual entrepreneur the spatial level is, the more impactful it is for well-being processes in terms of direct effects. Thereby one needs to assume that the macro-psychological environment may shape proximal or intra-individual stress and well-being mechanisms. In terms of moderating effects, it could well be that broader levels can show a similarly important effect like levels that are more proximal to the individual entrepreneur. But it is up to future research to test the link between macro-psychology, on the one hand, and subjective and psychological well-being and mental health in entrepreneurs, on the other, at various spatial levels.

7.12 NEW DATA METHODS AND CHALLENGES: BIG DATA AND AI

Future research in the field of geographical entrepreneurial psychology can greatly benefit from new types of data and methodological advances – advances in the generation and analysis of data that not only helps in mapping the geography of entrepreneurial psychology across various spatial levels, but also enables a more focused study of relevant region-level mechanisms, which is currently a great methodological challenge in the field. How can we gather reliable data that capture macro-psychological factors and dynamics – the classic "something in the air" question – in regional economics that is so hard to answer empirically (Marshall 1920; Saxenian 1996)?

New generations of big data and AI methods come with promising potential to help address these fundamental questions (Kosinski et al. 2015; Obschonka 2017; Obschonka and Audretsch 2020; Obschonka et al. 2020a, 2020b). For example, macro-psychological information extracted from social media can be an important data source for geographical entrepreneurial psychology. It is possible to apply micro-level psychological concepts (e.g., personality trait taxonomies) and then use AI-based psychometric text analysis (Boyd and

Pennebaker 2017) to translate text patterns used in social media in a given location into region-level personality traits that can help explain geographical differences in entrepreneurial activity (Obschonka et al. 2020a). Many other data sources can serve as a starting point for future empirical projects addressing the geography of entrepreneurial psychology, for example psychological information in big behavioral data (Boyd et al. 2020), including sophisticated analyses of digital footprints of millions of people collected by large online platforms such as Google or Facebook while being online or in proximity to connected devices (e.g., Obradovich et al. 2020). Without a doubt, such new types of data and AI-supported analyses will be one of the major drivers of progress in geographical psychology.

Despite these great promises of a new data era, future studies need to be mindful of the potential limitations and pitfalls associated with big data and AI (Obschonka and Audretsch 2020; Schwab and Zhang 2018). For example, in view of a flood of data (e.g., social media, large internet-based studies, internet platforms collecting large amounts of data from customers and users; Kosinski et al. 2015, 2016) it might be particularly important for entrepreneurship research to ensure research rigor and relevance (Wiklund, Wright and Zahra 2019), and a close link to entrepreneurship theories as well as testing enabled by AI-supported research methods (Lévesque et al. 2020). Also, important ethical issues need careful consideration when dealing with such types of data (Boyd et al. 2020; Jobin et al. 2019; Kosinski et al. 2015).

Finally, the field relies on the integration of statistical advances to ensure research rigor and to deal with the special nature of macro-psychological data (Ebert et al. 2019a). Such challenges in these data include spatial autocorrelation, multi-level analyses and causation. Spatial autocorrelation occurs if there is systematic spatial variation between closely situated regions. For example, neighboring regions can have relatively similar levels in macro-psychological variables.

This positive spatial correlation is often a sign of a potentially interesting interrelation or similarity between both regions (Anselin and Griffith 1988). With respect to entrepreneurship rates, the populace of both regions might have extensive contact with each other that led to the formation of a shared entrepreneurial mindset in both regions which materializes in quite similar scores in several entrepreneurship-relevant psychological characteristics. Another reason for positive correlation in entrepreneurship-relevant personality characteristics might simply be the fact that both regions belong to the same state and that statewide entrepreneurship-friendly policies might have impacted the mindset of the populace in both regions.

While spatial autocorrelation can be detected with the appropriate econometric tools, there are several ways to deal with it. Thereby, it is important to note that spatial autocorrelation is not always a problem, but can also be of interest in itself (Getis 2007). A case in point is the above described contact between the populace of two regions where the interested researcher could test how strong the ties between both regions are and thus their mutual impact. In the case of similarities between the regions due to belonging to the same state, one can use state-fixed effects in a sample of several regions belonging to several states to control for the higher-level state effects.

Multi-level analysis can become an important tool for the geography of entrepreneurial psychology because individuals act in contexts making individual- as well as regional-level variables predictors of entrepreneurship. This very book rests on the premise that individual-level psychological characteristics affect individual entrepreneurship but also that its regional level aggregates affect regional entrepreneurship. Even more interesting are cross-level interaction; for instance, the effect of the individual Big Five variables on entrepreneurship depends to some degree on the regional Big Five values (such as described in Chapter 7.10) on the micro–macro effect of agreeableness on entrepreneurial success (Zhou et al. 2019). Multi-level analysis is quite common in entrepreneurship but its potential is far from exhausted. This type of analysis, however, runs into problems if there are too few observations at one or both levels (Snijders and Bosker 1999); but also too many level 1 observations can pose a challenge to researchers as computational power to run some specific multi-level analysis can be too low.

Causality as the relation between cause and effect is at the heart of the knowledge generation process in many sciences. Especially in economics, the use of econometric strategies to detect causal effects has progressed steadily since the application of experiments. Beside laboratory experiments, economists also exploit natural experiments, instrumental variable techniques and difference in difference settings (Varian 2016). In entrepreneurship, the use of causality identifying methods is still relatively limited and often stems from scholars with an economics background (e.g., Bauernschuster 2010). However, we see more and more entrepreneurship studies using experimental designs (Hsu et al. 2017), which, however, can face trade-offs between external and construct validity (Grégoire et al. 2019).

Psychological research is often confronted with a particular challenge to establish causality in psychological processes that are hard to measure, and where it is difficult to isolate cause and effect. However, employing more causal methods has also become a key strategy in modern psychological research, not only via well-designed experiments but also via methods such as sophisticated longitudinal study designs (Usami et al. 2019), intervention studies (Bolier et al. 2013), mediation analyses (Nguyen et al. 2020) and observational studies employing econometric causal methods such as the instrumental variable approach (Maydeu-Olivares et al. 2020).

With respect to the field of geographical psychology, the use of natural experiments, instrumental variables and difference in difference settings provides great promise to advance our knowledge into the determinants and effects of differences in psychological characteristics. An example of the first two was described in Chapter 5 where Stuetzer et al. (2016) used the regional distribution of the coalfields in Great Britain as a natural experiment when studying the impact of the historic industry structure on contemporary entrepreneurship rates and the regional entrepreneurial personality profile. As the regional industry structure and the mindset of the regional population probably co-influence each other, the authors used coal availability as a surrogate for a large-scale industry structure. In other words, the coalfields were an instrumental variable that can only affect the regional entrepreneurial mindset of the population through its association with the large-scale industry structure. It is up to the researchers in the field of geographical psychology to look for and exploit such natural experiments in order to move beyond correlations. However, we caution against the sole focus of geographical psychology on this empirical endeavor. As a young research stream it is equally or even more important to invest in theory-building. Related to this, not every new theoretical approach can be tested immediately with causal methods. Potentially interesting new approaches should be thus considered first and not immediately scorched in the fires of causality.

8. Summary and outlook

This book has provided an overview over the new field of geography of entrepreneurial psychology, framed as an interdisciplinary research endeavor that bridges different perspectives, mostly from subdisciplines in psychology, geography and economics. Conceptually, the geography of entrepreneurial psychology is based on micro-foundations of the psychology of entrepreneurship at the individual level. It applies these concepts and constructs at the geographical level (e.g., regional personality differences), but also adds an important macro-psychological perspective that highlights regional psychological mechanisms that *truly* operate at the regional level (e.g., collective attitudes or norms, regional psychological climate or a psychological "herd mentality" of local populations, for example in terms of opportunity recognition; Gaglio and Katz 2001).

In the introduction to this book we illustrated the relevance of the geography of entrepreneurial psychology by referring to the popular concepts of "a vivid start-up culture", which has emerged as a key theme for policymakers, educators, business leaders, venture capitalists and entrepreneurs since the early 1990s. Specifically, we asked: But what is "a vivid start-up culture"? What are its key components? Can it be developed or is it simply a by-product of regional wealth and "economic muscles"? And what is the people side of "a vivid start-up culture"? The book delivers first answers to these questions, and we hope it will inspire a next generation of research in this field, as outlined in our suggestion for a future research agenda in Chapter 7. This future research could make important contributions not only to entrepreneurship research, but also to the broader fields of geographical psychology and economic geography. Whereas contributions to entrepreneurship research can address and highlight the need to understand more fully the macro-psychological factors and mechanisms driving concrete entrepreneurial outcomes and vice versa, contributions to geographical psychology can deliver more generalizable insights into the macro-psychology of whole regions and places and how this interacts with local economic behaviors. Contributions to economics geography could focus on the role of space as well as more conceptual and empirical clarity around soft factors in regional entrepreneurship, including the abstract umbrella concept of culture.

We find it also interesting to highlight that one of the central messages of this book is that while entrepreneurship is often depicted as a highly *individualized* phenomenon – as the pinnacle of what the concept of the American Dream describes as *individual* aspiration and freedom, it should also be seen as a *collective* phenomenon, shaped by the collective psychological environment. Growing research evidence shows that collective psychological factors and mechanisms do matter for individual entrepreneurship and it is thus important to emphasize that psychological approaches are not only useful to understand entrepreneurial individuals, but also whole regions and their collective economic vitality. Psychological approaches that, in turn, restrict their focus on individual self-optimization and intrapsychic mechanisms may not capture fully this collective aspect, and, more broadly, the human nature that fundamentally values, and strives for, not only autonomy but also relatedness and a sense of social identity (Deci and Ryan 2000; Tajfel 2010).

The geography of entrepreneurial psychology puts a special focus on the *spatial* components and mechanisms of entrepreneurship *and* entrepreneurial psychology as the subject of conceptual and empirical research. In other words, the conceptual and empirical integration of space into the psychology of entrepreneurship is one of the major aims of the geography of entrepreneurial psychology. A major proposition and promise in this field is that only if we take the psychological space seriously can we come to a fuller understanding of entrepreneurship, and of the psychological factors and mechanisms driving entrepreneurship and vice versa.

In doing so, we will also be able to better understand historical origins and processes that have contributed to the emergence and persistence of spatial differences in entrepreneurship. Applying a macro-psychological lens can deliver new research insights into the role of history and culture for present-day and future geographical patterns of entrepreneurship. As stressed earlier, it will also be interesting to ask how today's major developments in industry, business and society will transform the macro-psychological landscape. The digital revolution might not only transform and change the real-world phenomenon of entrepreneurship and the world of work in general, but also the role of psychology not only at the individual level but also at the geographical level. Can technological advances compensate for a more non-entrepreneurial macro-psychological profile in certain regions when for example AI-driven smart entrepreneurship would replace human agency as the key ingredient in the entrepreneurial process? Can regions where the local psychology is less conducive to entrepreneurship also become vibrant start-up hubs due to this change?

At least for the next decade or so, we can be quite certain that regional psychological differences and mechanisms will continue to play an important role for geographical patterns of entrepreneurship and the growth of regions. But we have to see if entrepreneurial algorithms and machine intelligence can, without the help of entrepreneurial humans, start and grow new businesses, which might replace entrepreneurs at some point in the future. This might also replace our strong attention to the vibrant start-up culture since such soft factors like culture might not matter to algorithms and machines. But as long as entrepreneurship needs human agency, the interplay between psychology and space will continue to be a fascinating, highly relevant research field that offers deep insights into local entrepreneurial mentalities and the psychological climate of regions and place associated with entrepreneurship. From this perspective, we can apply Alfred Marshall's (1920) description of the important intellectual spillovers in industry agglomerations – that something is "in the air" – to the psychology of regions and places independent if they represent an industry agglomeration or not.

Also macro-psychological factors and mechanisms of regions and places, not only intellectual spillovers, may represent the special something that is in the air. Even more importantly, macro-psychological factors and mechanisms could interact with intellectual spillovers in characteristic ways. Hence, what is *really* in the air might be the unique local interplay between macro-psychology and the generation and flow of ideas and knowledge (Obschonka et al. 2015). This could also be the *actual* core component of a vivid start-up culture, besides the actual entrepreneurial activity and performance in a given region or place.

However, it is now up to future research efforts to test these fascinating questions and assumptions with comprehensive, innovative data and interdisciplinary approaches. Until we have more causal evidence and more illustrative case studies, caution is required to avoid premature conclusions about mechanisms and concrete implications. We thus hope this book contributes to and further stimulates the intellectual journey and the research rigor that together will continue to develop the geography of entrepreneurial psychology into a more mature research field, with concrete implications for practice and policy.

References

Abdellaoui, A., Hugh-Jones, D., Yengo, L., Kemper, K. E., Nivard, M. G., Veul, L., Holtz, Y., Zietsch, B. P., Frayling, T. M., Wray, N. T., Yang, J., Verweij, K. J. H., & Visscher, P. M. (2019). Genetic correlates of social stratification in Great Britain. *Nature Human Behaviour*, *3*, 1332–42.

Acemoglu, D., & Robinson, J. A. (2012). *Why Nations Fail: The Origins of Power, Prosperity, and Poverty*. Washington, DC: Crown Books.

Acs, Z. J., & Audretsch, D. B. (1988). Innovation in large and small firms: an empirical analysis. *American Economic Review*, *78*(4), 678–90.

Acs, Z. J., Audretsch, D. B., & Evans, D. S. (1994). Why does the self-employment rate vary across countries and over time? *CERP Discussion Paper*, 871, Centre for Economic Policy Research.

Acs, Z. J., Braunerhjelm, P., Audretsch, D. B., & Carlsson, B. (2009). The knowledge spillover theory of entrepreneurship. *Small Business Economics*, *32*(1), 15–30.

Acs, Z. J., & Mueller, P. (2008). Employment effects of business dynamics: mice, gazelles and elephants. *Small Business Economics*, *30*, 85–100.

Acs, Z. J., Stam, E., Audretsch, D. B., & O'Connor, A. (2017). The lineages of the entrepreneurial ecosystem approach. *Small Business Economics*, *49*(1), 1–10.

Alesina, A., Guilano, P., & Nunn, N. (2011). Fertility and the plough. *American Economic Review*, *101*(3), 499–503.

Allport, G. W. (1923). The Leipzig Congress of Psychology. *American Journal of Psychology*, *34*, 612–15.

Amabile, T. M., Barsade, S. G., Mueller, J. S., & Staw, B. M. (2005). Affect and creativity at work. *Administrative Science Quarterly*, *50*(3), 367–403.

American Psychological Association (2017). *Ethical Principles of Psychologists and Code of Conduct*. Available at https://www.apa .org/ethics/code/.

Andersen, K. V., & Lorenzen, M. (2005). *The Geography of the Danish Creative Class: A Mapping and Analysis*. Copenhagen: Samfundslitteratur.

Andersson, M., & Koster, S. (2011). Sources of persistence in regional start-up rates: evidence from Sweden. *Journal of Economic Geography, 11*(1), 179–201.

Anselin, L., & Griffith, D. A. (1988). Do spatial effects really matter in regressin analysis? *Papers in Regional Science, 65*(1), 11–34.

Antonakis, J. (2017). On doing better science: from thrill of discovery to policy implications. *The Leadership Quarterly, 28*(1), 5–21.

Asendorpf, J. B., & van Aken, M. A. G. (1999). Resilient, overcontrolled and undercontrolled personality prototypes in childhood: replicability, predictive power, and the trait-type issue. *Journal of Personality and Social Psychology, 77*, 815–32.

Asheim, B., & Hansen, H. K. (2009). Knowledge bases, talents, and contexts: on the usefulness of the creative class approach in Sweden. *Economic Geography, 85*(4), 425–42.

Ashraf, Q., & Galor, O. (2013). The "Out of Africa" hypothesis, human genetic diversity, and comparative economic development. *American Economic Review, 103*(1), 1–46.

Audretsch, D.B., & Fritsch, M. (1994). On the measurement of entry rates. *Empirica, 21*, 105–13.

Audretsch, D. B., Grilo, I., & Thurik, A. R. (eds.) (2007). *Handbook of Research on Entrepreneurship Policy*. Cheltenham, UK and Northampton, MA, USA: Edward Elgar Publishing.

Audretsch, D. B., & Keilbach, M. (2004). Does entrepreneurship capital matter? *Entrepreneurship Theory and Practice, 28*(5), 419–29.

Audretsch, D. B., Lehmann, E. E., & Seitz, N. (2019). Amenities, subcultures, and entrepreneurship. *Small Business Economics, 56*, 571–91. Available at https://doi.org/10.1007/s11187-019-00190 -5.

Audretsch, D. B., Obschonka, M., Gosling, S. D., & Potter, J. (2017). A new perspective on entrepreneurial regions: linking cultural identity with latent and manifest entrepreneurship. *Small Business Economics, 48*(3), 681–97.

Audretsch, D. B., & Thurik, A. R. (2001). What's new about the new economy? Sources of growth in the managed and entrepreneurial economies. *Industrial and Corporate Change, 10*(1), 267–315.

Baltes, M. M., & Baltes, P. B. (eds.) (2014). *The Psychology of Control and Aging (Psychology Revivals)*. London: Psychology Press.

Baltes, P. B., Lindenberger, U., & Staudinger, U. M. (2007). Life span theory in developmental psychology. *Handbook of Child Psychology, Vol. 1: Theoretical Models of Human Development*, 6th edition, 569–664. Available at https://doi.org/10.1002/9780470147658.chpsy0111.

Bandura, A., Freeman, W. H., & Lightsey, R. (1999). *Self-Efficacy: The Exercise of Control*. New York: W. H. Freeman.

Bathelt, H., & Glückler, J. (2003). Toward a relational economic geography. *Journal of Economic Geography, 3*(2), 117–44.

Bauernschuster, S. (2010). *Empirical Strategies in Entrepreneurship and Innovation Research*. Faculty of Economics and Business Administration. Jena: Friedrich Schiller University.

Baumeister, R. (2003). The psychology of irrationality: why people make foolish, self-defeating choices. In I. Brocas & J. D. Carillo (eds.), *The Psychology of Economic Decisions, Vol. 1: Rationality and Well-Being*, 3–16. Oxford: Oxford University Press.

Baumol, W. J. (1968). Entrepreneurship in economic theory. *American Economic Review, 58*(2), 64–71.

Baumol, W. J. (1990). Entrepreneurship: productive, unproductive, and destructive. *Journal of Political Economy, 98*(5), 893–921.

Baycan-Levent, T., & Nijkamp, P. (2009). Characteristics of migrant entrepreneurship in Europe. *Entrepreneurship and Regional Development, 21*(4), 375–97.

Beaudry, C., & Schiffauerova, A. (2009). Who's right, Marshall or Jacobs? The localization versus urbanization debate. *Research Policy, 38*(2), 318–37.

Becker, G. S. (1976). *The Economic Approach to Human Behavior*. Chicago, IL: University of Chicago Press.

Becker, S. O., Horning, E., & Woessmann, L. (2011). Education and catch-up in the Industrial Revolution. *American Economic Journal: Macroeconomics, 3*(3), 92–126.

Becker, S. O., & Woessmann, L. (2009). Was Weber wrong? A human capital theory of Protestant economic history. *The Quarterly Journal of Economics, 124*(2), 531–96.

Bellanca, J. A. (ed.) (2010). *21st Century Skills: Rethinking How Students Learn*. Bloomington, IN: Solution Tree Press.

Benjamin, Jr., L. T. (2018). *A Brief History of Modern Psychology*. Hoboken, NJ: John Wiley & Sons.

Berry, J. W., Poortinga, Y. H., Segall, M. H., & Dasen, P. R. (1992). *Cross-Cultural Psychology: Research and Applications.* New York: Cambridge University Press.

Beugelsdijk, S. (2007). Entrepreneurial culture, regional innovativeness and economic growth. *Journal of Evolutionary Economics*, *17*, 187–210.

Beugelsdijk, S., & Maseland, R. (2011). *Culture in Economics: History, Methodological Reflections and Contemporary Applications.* Cambridge: Cambridge University Press.

Beugelsdijk, S., & Smeets, R. (2008). Entrepreneurial culture and economic growth: revisiting McClelland's thesis. *American Journal of Economics and Sociology*, *67*(5), 915–39.

Beugelsdijk, S., & Welzel, C. (2018). Dimensions and dynamics of national culture: synthesizing Hofstede with Inglehart. *Journal of Cross-Cultural Psychology*, *49*(10), 1469–505.

Birch, D. (1979). *The Job Generation Process*. MIT program on neighborhood and regional change. Cambridge, MA: MIT Press.

Bleakley, H., & Lin, J. (2012). Portage and path dependence. *Quarterly Journal of Economics*, *127*, 587–644.

Bleidorn, W., Hill, P. L., Back, M. D., Denissen, J. J., Hennecke, M., Hopwood, C. J., … & Orth, U. (2019). The policy relevance of personality traits. *American Psychologist*, *74*(9), 1056–67.

Bleidorn, W., Hopwood, C. J., & Lucas, R. E. (2018). Life events and personality trait change. *Journal of Personality*, *86*(1), 83–96.

Bleidorn, W., Schönbrodt, F., Gebauer, J. E., Rentfrow, P. J., Potter, J., & Gosling, S. D. (2016). To live among like-minded others: exploring the links between person-city personality fit and self-esteem. *Psychological Science*, *27*(3), 419–27.

Block, J. (1971). *Lives Through Times.* Berkeley, CA: Bancroft.

Bolier, L., Haverman, M., Westerhof, G. J., Riper, H., Smit, F., & Bohlmeijer, E. (2013). Positive psychology interventions: a meta-analysis of randomized controlled studies. *BMC Public Health*, *13*(119), 1–20. Available at https://doi.org/10.1186/1471-2458-13-119.

Boschma, R., & Fritsch, M. (2009). Creative class and regional growth: empirical evidence from seven European countries. *Economic Geography*, *85*, 391–423.

Bosma, N. (2013). The Global Entrepreneurship Monitor (GEM) and its impact on entrepreneurship research. *Foundations and Trends® in Entrepreneurship*, *9*(2), 143–248.

Bosma, N., Hessels, J., Schutjens, V., Van Praag, M., & Verheul, I. (2012). Entrepreneurship and role models. *Journal of Economic Psychology*, *33*, 410–24.

Boyd, R., & Richerson, P. J. (2005). *The Origin and Evolution of Cultures*. Oxford: Oxford University Press.

Boyd, R. L., Pasca, P., & Lanning, K. (2020). The personality panorama: conceptualizing personality through big behavioural data. *European Journal of Personality*, *34*(5), 599–612.

Boyd, R. L., & Pennebaker, J. W. (2017). Language-based personality. *Current Opinion in Behavioral Sciences*, *18*, 63–8.

Braun, S., & Kvasnicka, M. (2014). Immigration and structural change: evidence from post-war Germany. *Journal of International Economics*, *93*, 253–69.

Brezinski, H. (1987). The second economy in the GDR: pragmatism is gaining ground. *Studies in Comparative Communism*, *20*, 85–101.

Brixy, U., & Grotz, R. (2007). Regional patterns and determinants of birth and survival of new firms in Western Germany. *Entrepreneurship & Regional Development*, *19*, 293–312.

Bronfenbrenner, U. (1979). The ecology of human development: experiments by nature and design. Cambridge, MA: Harvard University Press.

Brüderl, J., Preisendörfer, P., & Ziegler, R. (1992). Survival chances of newly founded business organizations. *American Sociological Review*, *57*(2), 227–42.

Brynjolfsson, E., & McAfee, A. (2014). *The Second Machine Age: Work, Progress, and Prosperity in a Time of Brilliant Technologies*. New York: W. W. Norton & Company.

Busenitz, L. W., & Barney, J. B. (1997). Differences between entrepreneurs and managers in large organizations: biases and heuristics in strategic decision-making. *Journal of Business Venturing*, *12*(1), 9–30.

Camerer, C. F., & Loewenstein, G. (2003). Behavioral economics: past, present, future. In C. F. Camerer, G. Loewenstein, & M. Rabin (eds.), *Advances in Behavioral Economics*, 1–61. Roundtable series in behavioral economics. Princeton, NJ: Princeton University Press.

Campbell, P. (2019). Dispositional traits and internal migration: personality as a predictor of migration in Australia. *Journal of Research in Personality*, *78*, 262–7.

Campos, F., Frese, M., Goldstein, M., Iacovone, L., Johnson, H. C., McKenzie, D., & Mensmann, M. (2017). Teaching personal initiative beats traditional training in boosting small business in West Africa. *Science*, *357*(6357), 1287–90.

Cantoni, D., Cheng, Y., Yang, D. Y., Yuchtman, N., & Zhang, Y. L. (2017). Curriculum and ideology. *Journal of Political Economy*, *125*(2), 338–92.

Cantoni, D., & Yuchtman, N. (2014). Medieval universities, legal institutions, and the commercial revolution. *The Quarterly Journal of Economics*, *129*(2), 823–87.

Caragliu, A., de Dominicis, L., & de Groot, H. L. (2016). Both Marshall and Jacobs were right! *Economic Geography*, *92*(1), 87–111.

Caragliu, A., Del Bo, C. F., Kourtit, K., & Nijkamp, P. (2016). The winner takes it all: forward-looking cities and urban innovation. *Annals of Regional Science*, *56*(3), 617–45.

Cartwright, E. (2018). *Behavioral Economics*. 3rd edition. Abingdon: Routledge.

Caspi, A., & Roberts, B. W. (2001). Personality development across the life course: the argument for change and continuity. *Psychological Inquiry*, *12*(2), 49–66.

Casson, M., & Casson, C. (2014). The history of entrepreneurship: medieval origins of a modern phenomenon. *Business History*, *56*(8), 1223–42.

Cervone, D., & Shoda, Y. (1999). Beyond traits in the study of personality coherence. *Current Directions in Psychological Science*, *8*, 27–32.

Chapman, B. P., & Goldberg, L. R. (2011). Replicability and 40-year predictive power of childhood ACR-types. *Journal of Personality and Social Psychology*, *101*, 593–606.

Chinitz, B. (1961). Contrasts in agglomeration: New York and Pittsburgh. *American Economic Review*, *51*(2), 279–89.

Chlosta, S., Patzelt, H., Klein, S. B., & Dormann C. (2012). Parental role models and the decision to become self-employed: the moderating effect of personality. *Small Business Economics*, *38*, 121–38.

Cicchetti, D., & Rogosch, F. A. (1996). Equifinality and multifinality in developmental psychopathology. *Development and Psychopathology*, *8*(4), 597–600.

Coad, A. (2014). Death is not a success: reflections on business exit. *International Small Business Journal*, *32*, 721–32.

Cohen, S., & Wills, T. A. (1985). Stress, social support, and the buffering hypothesis. *Psychological Bulletin*, *98*(2), 310–57.

Coleman, J. S. (1988). Social capital in the creation of human capital. *American Journal of Sociology (Supplement)*, *94*, 95–120.

Collins, C. J., Hanges, P. J., & Locke, E. A. (2004). The relationship of achievement motivation to entrepreneurial behavior: a meta-analysis. *Human Performance*, *17*(1), 95–117.

Cornelissen, J. P. (2005). Beyond compare: metaphor in organization theory. *Academy of Management Review*, *30*(4), 751–64.

Cronbach, L. J., & Gleser, G. C. (1953). Assessing the similarity between profiles. *Psychological Bulletin, 50,* 456–73.

Cunha, F., Heckman, J. J., Lochner, L., & Masterov, D. V. (2006). Interpreting the evidence on life cycle skill formation. In E. Hanushek & F. Welch (eds.), *Handbook of the Economics of Education, Vol. 1,* 697–812. Amsterdam: North Holland.

Curini, L., Iacus, S., & Canova, L. (2015). Measuring idiosyncratic happiness through the analysis of twitter: an application to the Italian case. *Social Indicators Research, 121*(2), 525–42.

Dalgaard, C.-J., Kaarsen, N., Olsson, O., & Selaya, P. (2018). Roman roads to prosperity: persistence and non-persistence of public goods provision (mimeo).

Davidsson, P. (1995). Culture, structure and regional levels of entreprenuership. *Entrepreneurship & Regional Development, 7*(1), 41–62.

Davidsson, P. (2007). Method challenges and opportunities in the psychological study of entrepreneurship. In J. R. Baum, M. Frese, & R. A. Baron (eds.), *The Psychology of Entrepreneurship,* 287–323. Mahwah, NJ: Erlbaum.

Davidsson, P. (2016a). A "business researcher" view on opportunities for psychology in entrepreneurship research. *Applied Psychology, 65*(3), 628–36.

Davidsson, P. (2016b). *Researching Entrepreneurship: Conceptualization and Design.* New York: Springer.

Davidsson, P., & Honig, B. (2003). The role of social and human capital among nascent entrepreneurs. *Journal of Business Venturing, 18*(3), 301–31.

Davidsson, P., & Wiklund, J. (1997). Values, beliefs and regional variations in new firm formation rates. *Journal of Economic Psychology, 18,* 179–99.

Davis, D. R., & Weinstein, D. E. (2002). Bones, bombs, and break points: the geography of economic activity. *American Economic Review, 92*(5), 1269–89.

de Groot, H. L., Poot, J., & Smit, M. J. (2016). Which agglomeration externalities matter most and why? *Journal of Economic Surveys, 30*(4), 756–82.

Deci, E. L., & Ryan, R. M. (2000). The "what" and "why" of goal pursuits: human needs and the self-determination of behavior. *Psychological Inquiry, 11,* 227–68.

Denzau, A. T., & North, D. C. (1994). Shared mental models: ideologies and institutions. *Kyklos, 47*(1), 3–31.

Dheer, R. J. S. (2017). Cross-national differences in entrepreneurial activity: role of culture and institutional factors. *Small Business Economics*, *48*(4), 813–42.

Dittmar, J. E. (2011). Information technology and economic change: the impact of the printing press. *Quarterly Journal of Economics*, *126*(3), 1133–72.

Doern, R. (2016). Entrepreneurship and crisis management: the experiences of small businesses during the London 2011 riots. *International Small Business Journal*, *34*(3), 276–302.

Dohmen, T., Falk, A., Huffman, D., & Sunde, U. (2012). The inter-generational transmission of risk and trust attitudes. *Review of Economic Studies*, *79*, 645–77.

Dubini, P. (1989). The influence of motivations and environment on business start-ups: some hints for public policies. *Journal of Business Venturing*, *4*, 11–26.

Ebert, T., Gebauer, J. E., Brenner, T., Bleidorn, W., Gosling, S. D., Potter, J., & Rentfrow, P. J. (2019a). *Are Regional Differences in Personality and their Correlates Robust? Applying Spatial Analysis Techniques to Examine Regional Variation in Personality across the US and Germany* (No. 2019-05). Philipps University Marburg: Department of Geography.

Ebert, T., Gebauer, J. E., Talman, J. R., & Rentfrow, P. J. (2020). Religious people only live longer in religious cultural contexts: a gravestone analysis. *Journal of Personality and Social Psychology*, *119*(1), 1–6.

Ebert, T., Götz, F. M., Obschonka, M., Zmigrod, L., & Rentfrow, P. J. (2019b). Regional variation in courage and entrepreneurship: the contrasting role of courage for the emergence and survival of start-ups in the United States. *Journal of Personality*, *87*(5), 1039–55.

Eccles, J. S., & Wigfield, A. (2002). Motivational beliefs, values, and goals. *Annual Review of Psychology*, *53*, 109–32.

Efferson, C., Lalive, R., & Fehr, E. (2008). The coevolution of cultural groups and ingroup favoritism. *Science*, *321*(5897), 1844–9.

Eichstaedt, J. C., Schwartz, H. A., Kern, M. L., Park, G., Labarthe, D. R., Merchant, R. M., ... & Weeg, C. (2015). Psychological language on Twitter predicts county-level heart disease mortality. *Psychological Science*, *26*(2), 159–69.

Eisenhardt, K. M., & Graebner, M. E. (2007). Theory building from cases: opportunities and challenges. *Academy of Management Journal*, *50*(1), 25–32.

Elder, Jr., G. H. (1999). *Children of the Great Depression: Social Change in Life Experience*. Boulder, CO: Westview Press.

Elfenbein, D. W., Hamilton, B. H., & Zenger, T. R. (2010). The small firm effect and the entrepreneurial spawning of scientists and engineers. *Management Science*, *56*(4), 659–81.

Elleman, L. G., Condon, D. M., Russin, S. E., & Revelle, W. (2018). The personality of US states: stability from 1999 to 2015. *Journal of Research in Personality*, *72*, 64–72.

Etzioni, A. (1987). Entrepreneurship, adaptation and legitimation: a macro-behavioral perspective. *Journal of Economic Behavior & Organization*, *8*(2), 175–89.

Falck, O., Fritsch, M., & Heblich, S. (2011). The phantom of the opera: cultural amenities, human capital, and regional economic growth. *Labour Economics*, *18*(6), 755–66.

Falck, O., Heblich, S., & Luedemann, E. (2012). Identity and entrepreneurship: do school peers shape entrepreneurial intentions? *Small Business Economics*, *39*(1), 39–59.

Fauchart, E., & Gruber, M. (2011). Darwinians, communitarians, and missionaries: the role of founder identity in entrepreneurship. *Academy of Management Journal*, *54*(5), 935–57.

Fay, D., & Frese, M. (2001). The concept of personal initiative: an overview of validity studies. *Human Performance*, *14*(1), 97–124.

Fayolle, A. (ed.) (2018). *A Research Agenda for Entrepreneurship Education*. Cheltenham, UK and Northampton, MA, USA: Edward Elgar Publishing.

Feldman, M. P. (2001). The entrepreneurial event revisited: firm formation in a regional context. *Industrial and Corporate Change*, *10*(4), 861–91.

Fitjar, R. D., & Rodríguez-Pose, A. (2011). Innovating in the periphery: firms, values and innovation in southwest Norway. *European Planning Studies*, *19*(4), 555–74.

Florida, R. (2004). *The Rise of the Creative Class* (Vol. 9) [originally published 2002]. New York: Basic Books.

Florida, R. (2010). *Who's Your City? How the Creative Economy is Making Where to Live the Most Important Decision of Your Life*. New York: Basic Books.

Florida, R., Mellander, C., & Stolarick, K. (2008). Inside the black box of regional development—human capital, the creative class and tolerance. *Journal of Economic Geography*, *8*(5), 615–49.

Fornahl, D. (2003). Entrepreneurial activities in a regional context. In D. Fornahl & T. Brenner (eds.), *Cooperation, Networks and Institutions in Regional Innovation Systems*, 38–57. Cheltenham, UK and Northampton, MA, USA: Edward Elgar Publishing.

Fornahl, D. (2007). *Changes in Regional Firm Founding Activities: A Theoretical Explanation and Empirical Evidence*. London: Routledge.

Fotopoulos, G. (2014). On the spatial stickiness of UK new firm formation rates. *Journal of Economic Geography, 14*(3), 651–79.

Fotopoulos, G., & Storey, D. J. (2017). Persistence and change in interregional differences in entrepreneurship: England and Wales, 1921–2011. *Environment and Planning A, 49*(3), 670–702.

Fouarge, D., Özer, M. N., & Seegers, P. (2019). Personality traits, migration intentions, and cultural distance. *Papers in Regional Science, 98*(6), 2425–54.

Fouberg, E. H., & Murphy, A. B. (2020). *Human Geography: People, Place, and Culture*. Hoboken, NJ: John Wiley & Sons.

Freeman, K. B. (1976). The significance of McCelland's achievement variable in the aggregate production function. *Economic Development and Cultural Change, 24*, 815–24.

Frese, M. (1982). Occupational socialization and psychological development: an underemphasized research perspective in industrial psychology. *Journal of Occupational Psychology, 55*(3), 209–24.

Frese, M. (2009). *Toward a Psychology of Entrepreneurship: An Action Theory Perspective*. Delft: Now Publishers Inc.

Frese, M., Garst, H., & Fay, D. (2007). Making things happen: reciprocal relationships between work characteristics and personal initiative in a four-wave longitudinal structural equation model. *Journal of Applied Psychology, 92*(4), 1084–102.

Frese, M., & Gielnik, M. M. (2014). The psychology of entrepreneurship. *Annu. Rev. Organ. Psychol. Organ. Behav., 1*(1), 413–38.

Frese, M., Kring, W., Soose, A., & Zempel, J. (1996). Personal initiative at work: differences between East and West Germany. *Academy of Management Journal, 39*(1), 37–63.

Frese, M., & Zapf, D. (1994). Action as the core of work psychology: a German approach. *Handbook of Industrial and Organizational Psychology, 4*(2), 271–340.

Freytag, A., & Thurik, R. (2007). Entrepreneurship and its determinants in a cross-country setting. *Journal of Evolutionary Economics, 17*(2), 117–31.

Fritsch, M. (2013), New business formation and regional development: a survey and assessment of the evidence. *Foundations and Trends® in Entrepreneurship, 9*(3), 249–364.

Fritsch, M., & Aamoucke, R. (2017). Fields of knowledge in higher education institutions, and innovative start-ups: an empirical investigation. *Papers in Regional Science, 96*, S1–S27.

Fritsch, M., & Falck, O. (2007). New business formation by industry over space and time: a multidimensional analysis. *Regional Studies*, *41*(2), 157–72.

Fritsch, M., Kristalova, M., & Wyrwich, M. (2020). Regional trajectories of entrepreneurship: the effect of socialism and transition. Jena Economic Research Papers #2020-009, Jena: Friedrich Schiller University.

Fritsch, M., Kristalova, M., & Wyrwich, M. (2021). One transition story does not fit them all: initial regional conditions and new business formation after socialism. Post-Communist Economies (forthcoming).

Fritsch, M., & Kublina, S. (2019). Persistence and change of regional new business formation in the national league table. *Journal of Evolutionary Economics*, *29*, 891–917.

Fritsch, M., & Mueller, P. (2007). The persistence of regional new business formation-activity over time: assessing the potential of policy promotion programs. *Journal of Evolutionary Economics*, *17*(3), 299–315.

Fritsch, M., Obschonka, M., Wahl, F., & Wyrwich, M. (2020c). The deep imprint of Roman sandals: evidence of long-lasting effects of Roman rule on personality, economic performance, and well-being in Germany. Jena Economic Research Papers #2020-005, Jena: Friedrich Schiller University.

Fritsch, M., Obschonka M., & Wyrwich, M. (2019). Historical roots of entrepreneurial culture and innovation activity: an analysis for German regions. *Regional Studies*, *53*(9), 1296–307.

Fritsch, M., Pylak, K., & Wyrwich, M. (2019). Persistence of entrepreneurship in different historical contexts. Jena Economic Research Papers #2019-003, Jena: Friedrich Schiller University.

Fritsch, M., & Sorgner, A. (2014). Entrepreneurship and creative professions—a micro-level analysis. In R. Sternberg & G. Krauss (eds.), *Handbook of Research on Entrepreneurship and Creativity*, 145–74. Cheltenham, UK and Northampton, MA, USA: Edward Elgar Publishing.

Fritsch, M., Sorgner, A., Wyrwich, M., & Zazdravnykh, E. (2019). Historical shocks and persistence of economic activity: evidence on self-employment from a unique natural experiment. *Regional Studies*, *53*, 790–802.

Fritsch, M., & Storey, D. J. (2014). Entrepreneurship in a regional context: historical roots, recent developments and future challenges. *Regional Studies*, *48*, 939–54.

Fritsch, M., & Wyrwich, M. (2014). The long persistence of regional levels of entrepreneurship: Germany, 1925–2005. *Regional Studies*, *48*(6), 955–73.

Fritsch, M., & Wyrwich, M. (2016a). Does persistence in start-up activity reflect persistence in social capital? In H. Westlund & J. P. Larsson (eds.), *Handbook on Social Capital and Regional Development*, 82–107. Cheltenham, UK and Northampton, MA, USA: Edward Elgar Publishing.

Fritsch, M., & Wyrwich, M. (2016b). The persistence of regional entrepreneurship: are all types of self-employment equally important? In E. Mack & H. Qian (eds.), *Geographies of Entrepreneurship*, 48–67. Abindgdon: Routledge.

Fritsch, M., & Wyrwich, M. (2017a). The effect of entrepreneurship for economic development: an empirical analysis using regional entrepreneurship culture. *Journal of Economic Geography*, *17*, 157–89.

Fritsch, M., & Wyrwich, M. (2017b). Persistence of regional entrepreneurship: causes, effects, and directions for future research. *International Review of Entrepreneurship*, *15*(4), 395–416.

Fritsch, M., & Wyrwich, M. (2018). Regional knowledge, entrepreneurial culture and innovative start-ups over time and space—an empirical investigation. *Small Business Economics*, *51*, 337–53.

Fritsch, M., & Wyrwich, M. (2019). *Regional Trajectories of Entrepreneurship, Knowledge, and Growth: The Role of History and Culture*. Cham: Springer.

Fritsch, M., & Wyrwich, M. (2020). Initial conditions and regional performance after socialism: the case of East Germany. Jena: Friedrich Schiller University (mimeo).

Fujita, M., & Krugman, P. (2004). The new economic geography: past, present and the future. *Papers in Regional Science*, *83*(1), 139–64.

Funder, D.C., & Ozer, D. J. (2019). Evaluating effect size in psychological research: sense and nonsense. *Advances in Methods and Practices in Psychological Science*, *2*(2), 156–68.

Gaglio, C. M., & Katz, J. A. (2001). The psychological basis of opportunity identification: entrepreneurial alertness. *Small Business Economics*, *16*(2), 95–111.

Garretsen, H., Stoker, J. I., Soudis, D., Martin, R., & Rentfrow, P. J. (2018). The relevance of personality traits for urban economic growth: making space for psychological factors. *Journal of Economic Geography*, *19*(3), 541–65.

Garretsen, H., Stoker, J., Soudis, D., Martin, R., & Rentfrow, J. (2020). Urban psychology and British cities: do personality traits matter for resilience to recessions? *Journal of Urban Regeneration & Renewal, 13*(3), 290–307.

Gartner, W. B. (1988). "Who is an entrepreneur?" is the wrong question. *American Journal of Small Business, 12*(4), 11–32.

Geldhof, G. J., Weiner, M., Agans, J. P., Mueller, M. K., & Lerner, R. M. (2014). Understanding entrepreneurial intent in late adolescence: the role of intentional self-regulation and innovation. *Journal of Youth and Adolescence, 43*(1), 81–91.

Gelfand, M. J. (2019). Explaining the puzzle of human diversity. *Science, 366*(6466), 686–7.

Getis, A. (2007). Reflections on spatial autocorrelation. *Regional Science and Urban Economics, 37*(4), 491–6.

Gielnik, M. M., Spitzmuller, M., Schmitt, A., Klemann, D. K., & Frese, M. (2015). "I put in effort, therefore I am passionate": investigating the path from effort to passion in entrepreneurship. *Academy of Management Journal, 58*(4), 1012–31.

Gielnik, M. M., Zacher, H., & Wang, M. (2018). Age in the entrepreneurial process: the role of future time perspective and prior entrepreneurial experience. *Journal of Applied Psychology, 103*(10), 1067–85.

Gigerenzer, G. (2004). The irrationality paradox. *Behavioral and Brain Sciences, 27*(3), 336–8.

Gigerenzer, G., & Selten, R. (eds.) (2002). *Bounded Rationality: The Adaptive Toolbox*. Cambridge, MA: MIT Press.

Gilleard, C. J. (1989). The achieving society revisited: a further analysis of the relation between national economic growth and need achievement. *Journal of Economic Psychology, 10*(1), 21–34.

Giuliano, P., & Nunn, N. (2020). Understanding cultural persistence and change. *Review of Economic Studies*. Available at https://doi.org/10.1093/restud/rdaa074.

Glaeser, E. L. (2005). Review of Richard Florida's *The Rise of the Creative Class*. *Regional Science and Urban Economics. 35*(5), 593–6.

Glaeser, E. L. (2011). *Triumph of the City: How Urban Spaces Make Us Human*. London: Pan Macmillan.

Glaeser, E. L., Kallal, H. D., Scheinkman, J. A., & Shleifer, A. (1992). Growth in cities. *Journal of Political Economy, 100*(6), 1126–52.

Glaeser, E. L., Pekalla-Kerr, S., & Kerr, W. R. (2015). Entrepreneurship and urban growth: an empirical assessment with historical mines. *Review of Economics and Statistics, 97*(2), 498–520.

Gorgievski, M. J., & Stephan, U. (2016). Advancing the psychology of entrepreneurship: a review of the psychological literature and an introduction. *Applied Psychology, 65*(3), 437–68.

Gosling, S. D., Vazire, S., Srivastava, S., & John, O. P. (2004). Should we trust web-based studies? A comparative analysis of six preconceptions about internet questionnaires. *American Psychologist, 59*(2), 93–104.

Gottlieb, G. (2003). On making behavioral genetics truly developmental. *Human Development, 46*, 337–55.

Gottlieb, G. (2007). Probabilistic epigenesis. *Developmental Science, 10*(1), 1–11.

Götz, F. M., Ebert, T., & Rentfrow, P. J. (2018). Regional cultures and the psychological geography of Switzerland: person–environment–fit in personality predicts subjective well-being. *Frontiers in Psychology, 9,* 517. Available at https://www.frontiersin.org/articles/10.3389/fpsyg.2018.00517/full.

Götz, F. M., Stieger, S., Gosling, S. D., Potter, J., & Rentfrow, P. J. (2020). Physical topography is associated with human personality. *Nature Human Behaviour, 4*(11), 1–10.

Grégoire, D. A., Binder, J. K., & Rauch, A. (2019). Navigating the validity tradeoffs of entrepreneurship research experiments: a systematic review and best-practice suggestions. *Journal of Business Venturing, 34*(2), 284–310.

Gregory, D., & Walford, R. (eds.) (2016). *Horizons in Human Geography.* London: Macmillan International Higher Education.

Greif, A. (1994). Cultural beliefs and the organization of society: a historical and theoretical reflection on collectivist and individualist societies. *Journal of Political Economy, 102*(5), 912–50.

Greif, A. (2006). *Institutions and the Path to the Modern Economy: Lessons from Medieval Trade.* Cambridge: Cambridge University Press.

Griffin, P., & Care, E. (eds.) (2014). *Assessment and Teaching of 21st Century Skills: Methods and Approach.* Dordrecht: Springer.

Grillitsch, M. (2016). Institutions, smart specialisation dynamics and policy. *Environment and Planning C: Government and Policy, 34*(1), 22–37.

Guiso, L., Sapienza, P., & Zingales, L. (2006). Does culture affect economic outcomes? *Journal of Economic Perspectives, 20*(2), 23–48.

Gurven, M. D. (2018). Broadening horizons: sample diversity and socioecological theory are essential to the future of psychological science. *Proceedings of the National Academy of Sciences, 115*(45), 11420–7.

Guzman, J., & Stern, S. (2015). Where is Silicon Valley? *Science, 347*(6222), 606–9.

Hacker, W. (1998). *Allgemeine Arbeitspsychologie*. Bern: Huber.

Hausman, A., & Johnston, W. J. (2014). Timeline of a financial crisis: introduction to the special issue. *Journal of Business Research, 67*(1), 2667–70.

Hayton, J. C., & Cacciotti, G. (2013). Is there an entrepreneurial culture? A review of empirical research. *Entrepreneurship & Regional Development, 25*(9–10), 708–31.

Heckhausen, J., & Heckhausen, H. (eds.) (2008). *Motivation and Action* (Vol. 2). New York: Cambridge University Press.

Heckman, J. J. (2006). Skill formation and the economics of investing in disadvantaged children. *Science, 312*(5782), 1900–1902.

Henderson, J. V., Squires, T., Storeyguard, A., & Weil, D. (2018). The global distribution of economic activity: nature, history, and the role of trade. *Quarterly Journal of Economics, 133*(1), 357–406.

Hirst, W., Yamashiro, J. K., & Coman, A. (2018). Collective memory from a psychological perspective. *Trends in Cognitive Sciences, 22*(5), 438–51.

Hisrich, R., Langan-Fox, J., & Grant, S. (2007). Entrepreneurship research and practice: a call to action for psychology. *American Psychologist, 62*(6), 575–89.

Hoang, H., & Gimeno, J. (2010). Becoming a founder: how founder role identity affects entrepreneurial transitions and persistence in founding. *Journal of Business Venturing, 25*, 41–53.

Hobfoll, S. E. (1989). Conservation of resources: a new attempt at conceptualizing stress. *American Psychologist, 44*(3), 513–24.

Hobfoll, S. E. (2001). The influence of culture, community, and the nested-self in the stress process: advancing conservation of resources theory. *Applied Psychology, 50*(3), 337–421.

Hofstede, G. (2001). *Culture's Consequences: Comparing Values, Behaviors, Institutions, and Organizations Across Nations*. 2nd edition. Thousand Oaks, CA: Sage Publications.

Hofstede, G., Hofstede, G. J., & Minkov, M. (2010). *Cultures and Organizations: Software of the Mind*. New York: McGraw Hill.

Hofstede, G., & McCrae, R. R. (2004). Personality and culture revisited: linking traits and dimensions of culture. *Cross-Cultural Research, 38*(1), 52–88.

Hofstede, G., Noorderhaven, N., Thurik, R., Uhlaner, L. M., Wennekers, S., & Wildeman, R. E. (2004). Culture's role in entrepreneurship: self-employment out of dissatisfaction. In J. Ulijn & T. E. Brown (eds.), *Innovation, Entrepreneurship and Culture:*

The Interaction Between Technology, Progress and Economic Growth, 162–203. Cheltenham, UK and Northampton, MA, USA: Edward Elgar Publishing.

Hospers, G., & van Dalm, R. (2005). How to create a creative city? The viewpoints of Richard Florida and Jane Jacobs. *Foresight*, *7*(4), 8–12.

House, R. J., Hanges, P. J., Javidan, M., Dorfman, P. W., & Gupta, V. (2004). *Culture, Leadership and Organizations: The GLOBE Study of 62 societies*. Thousand Oaks, CA: Sage Publications.

Hsu, D. K., Simmons, S. A., & Wieland, A. M. (2017). Designing entrepreneurship experiments: a review, typology, and research agenda. *Organizational Research Methods*, *20*(3), 379–412.

Huber, L. R., Sloof, R., & Van Praag, M. (2014). The effect of early entrepreneurship education: evidence from a field experiment. *European Economic Review*, *72*, 76–97.

Huggins, R., & Thompson, P. (2019). The behavioural foundations of urban and regional development: culture, psychology and agency. *Journal of Economic Geography*, *19*(1), 121–46.

Huggins, R., Thompson, P., & Obschonka, M. (2018). Human behaviour and economic growth: a psychocultural perspective on local and regional development. *Environment and Planning A: Economy and Space*, *50*(6), 1269–89.

Jacobs, J. (1961). *The Death and Life of Great American Cities*. New York: Vintage Books.

Jacobs, J. (1969). *The Economy of Cities*. New York: Random House.

James, W. (1890). *Principles of Psychology* (Vols. 1–2). New York: Holt.

Jenkins, A. S., Wiklund, J., & Brundin, E. (2014). Individual responses to firm failure: appraisals, grief, and the influence of prior failure experience. *Journal of Business Venturing*, *29*(1), 17–33.

Jobin, A., Ienca, M., & Vayena, E. (2019). The global landscape of AI ethics guidelines. *Nature Machine Intelligence*, *1*(9), 389–99.

Jokela, M. (2009). Personality predicts migration within and between US states. *Journal of Research in Personality*, *43*(1), 79–83.

Jokela, M. (2014). Personality and the realization of migration desires. In P. J. Rentfrow (ed.), *Geographical Psychology: Exploring the Interaction of Environment and Behavior*, 71–87. Washington, DC: American Psychological Association.

Jokela, M. (2020). Selective residential mobility and social influence in the emergence of neighborhood personality differences: longitudinal data from Australia. *Journal of Research in Personality*, *86*. Available at https://doi.org/10.1016/j.jrp.2020.103953.

Jokela, M., Bleidorn, W., Lamb, M. E., Gosling, S. D., & Rentfrow, P. J. (2015). Geographically varying associations between personality and life satisfaction in the London metropolitan area. *Proceedings of the National Academy of Sciences, 112*(3), 725–30.

Jones, C., Lee, J. Y., & Lee, T. (2019). Institutionalizing place: materiality and meaning in Boston's north end. In P. Haack, J. Sieweke, & L. Wessel (eds.), *Microfoundations of Institutions*, 211–39. Bingley: Emerald Publishing.

Jones, M. J., Moore, S. R., & Kobor, M. S. (2018). Principles and challenges of applying epigenetic epidemiology to psychology. *Annual Review of Psychology, 69*, 459–85.

Judge, T. A., & Ilies, R. (2002). Relationship of personality to performance motivation: a meta-analytic review. *Journal of Applied Psychology, 87*(4), 797–807.

Kahneman, D. (2003). Maps of bounded rationality: psychology for behavioral economics. *American Economic Review, 93*(5), 1449–75.

Karlsson, C., Rickardsson, J., & Wincent, J. (2021). Diversity, innovation and entrepreneurship: where are we and where should we go in future studies? *Small Business Economics, 56*(2), 759–72. Available at https://doi.org/10.1007/s11187-019-00267-1.

Kashima, Y. (2016). Culture and psychology in the 21st century: conceptions of culture and person for psychology revisited. *Journal of Cross-Cultural Psychology, 47*(1), 4–20.

Kashima, Y., Bain, P. G., & Perfors, A. (2019). The psychology of cultural dynamics: what is it, what do we know, and what is yet to be known? *Annual Review of Psychology, 70*, 499–529.

Keller, H., & Greenfield, P. M. (2000). History and future of development in cross-cultural psychology. *Journal of Cross-Cultural Psychology, 31*(1), 52–62.

Kerr, S. P., Kerr, W. R., & Xu, T. (2018). Personality traits of entrepreneurs: a review of recent literature. *Foundations and Trends® in Entrepreneurship, 14*(3), 279–356.

Kibler, E., & Kautonen, T. (2016). The moral legitimacy of entrepreneurs: an analysis of early-stage entrepreneurship across 26 countries. *International Small Business Journal, 34*, 34–50.

Kibler, E., Kautonen, T., & Fink, M. (2014). Regional social legitimacy of entrepreneurship: implications for entrepreneurial intention and startup behaviour. *Regional Studies, 48*, 995–1015.

Kim, P. H., & Aldrich, H. E. (2005). Social capital and entrepreneurship. *Foundations and Trends® in Entrepreneurship, 1*(2), 55–104.

Kirchgässner, G. (2008). *Homo Oeconomicus: The Economic Model of Individual Behavior and its Applications in Economics and Other Social Sciences*. New York: Springer.

Kloosterman, R. C. (2010). Matching opportunities with resources: a framework for analysing (migrant) entrepreneurship from a mixed embeddedness perspective. *Entrepreneurship and Regional Development*, *22*(1), 25–45.

Klyver, K., Honig, B., & Steffens, P. (2018). Social support timing and persistence in nascent entrepreneurship: exploring when instrumental and emotional support is most effective. *Small Business Economics*, *51*(3), 709–34.

Knight, F. H. (1921). *Risk, Uncertainty, and Profit*. New York: Kelly & Millman.

Koellinger, P., Minniti, M., & Schade, C. (2007). "I think I can, I think I can": overconfidence and entrepreneurial behavior. *Journal of Economic Psychology*, *28*(4), 502–27.

Kohn, M. L., & Schooler, C. (1973). Occupational experience and psychological functioning: an assessment of reciprocal effects. *American Sociological Review*, *38*(1), 97–118.

Kohn, M. L., & Schooler, C. (1982). Job conditions and personality: a longitudinal assessment of their reciprocal effects. *American Journal of Sociology*, *87*, 1257–86.

Kosinski, M., Matz, S. C., Gosling, S. D., Popov, V., & Stillwell, D. (2015). Facebook as a research tool for the social sciences: opportunities, challenges, ethical considerations, and practical guidelines. *American Psychologist*, *70*(6), 543–56.

Kosinski, M., Stillwell, D., & Graepel, T. (2013). Private traits and attributes are predictable from digital records of human behavior. *Proceedings of the National Academy of Sciences*, *110*(15), 5802–5.

Kosinski, M., Wang, Y., Lakkaraju, H., & Leskovec, J. (2016). Mining big data to extract patterns and predict real-life outcomes. *Psychological Methods*, *21*(4), 493–506.

Krueger, N. F., Riley, M. D., & Carsrud, A. (2000). Competing models of entrepreneurial intentions. *Journal of Business Venturing*, *15*, 411–33.

Krugman, P. (2009). How did economists get it so wrong? New York Times Magazine, September 2. Available at http://www.nytimes.com/2009/09/06/magazine/06Economic-t.html.

Landes, D., Mokyr, J., & Baumol, W. J. (2010). *Invention of Enterprise: Entrepreneurship from Ancient Mesopotamia to Modern Times*. Princeton, NJ: Princeton University Press.

Landström, H. (2020). The evolution of entrepreneurship as a scholarly field. *Foundations and Trends® in Entrepreneurship, 16*(2), 65–243.

Landström, H., & Harirchi, G. (2018). The social structure of entrepreneurship as a scientific field. *Research Policy, 47*(3), 650–62.

Laspita, S., Breugst, N., Heblich, S., & Patzelt, P. (2012). Intergenerational transmission of entrepreneurial intentions. *Journal of Business Venturing, 27*, 414–35.

Lazear, E. P. (2005). Entrepreneurship. *Journal of Labor Economics, 23*(4), 649–80.

Lea, S. E. G., Tarpy, R. M., & Webley, P. (1987). *The Individual in the Economy: A Survey of Economic Psychology.* Cambridge: Cambridge University Press.

Lee, S. Y., Florida, R., & Acs, Z. (2004). Creativity and entrepreneurship: a regional analysis of new firm formation. *Regional Studies, 38*(8), 879–91.

Lee, Y. S. (2017). Entrepreneurship, small businesses and economic growth in cities. *Journal of Economic Geography, 17*(2), 311–43.

Lehman, D., Chiu, C. Y., & Schaller, M. (2004). Psychology and culture. *Annual Review of Psychology, 55*, 689–714.

Leontiev, A. N. (1978). *Activity, Consciousness, and Personality.* Englewood Cliffs, NJ: Prentice Hall.

Leontiev, A. N. (1981). *Problems of the Development of Mind.* Moscow: Progress Publishers.

Lerner, R. M. (1982). Children and adolescents as producers of their own development. *Developmental Review, 2*, 342–70.

Lévesque, M., Obschonka, M., & Nambisan, S. (2020). Pursuing impactful entrepreneurship research using artificial intelligence. *Entrepreneurship Theory and Practice.* Available at https://doi.org/10.1177/1042258720927369.

Lindquist, M., Sol, J., & van Praag, M. (2015). Why do entrepreneurial parents have entrepreneurial children? *Journal of Labour Economics, 33*, 269–96.

Locke, K., & Golden-Biddle, K. (1997). Constructing opportunities for contribution: structuring intertextual coherence and problematizing in organizational studies. *Academy of Management Journal, 40*(5), 1023–62.

Lönnqvist, J. E., Jasinskaja-Lahti, I., & Verkasalo, M. (2011). Personal values before and after migration: a longitudinal case study on value change in Ingrian–Finnish migrants. *Social Psychological and Personality Science, 2*(6), 584–91.

Lowe, R. A., & Ziedonis, A. A. (2006). Overoptimism and the performance of entrepreneurial firms. *Management Science, 52*(2), 173–86.

Lu, J. G. (2020). Air pollution: a systematic review of its psychological, economic, and social effects. *Current Opinion in Psychology, 32*, 52–65.

Magnusson, D., & Törestad, B. (1993). A holistic view of personality: a model revisited. *Annual Review of Psychology, 44*, 427–52.

Markus, H. R., & Kitayama, S. (1991). Culture and the self: implications for cognition, emotion, and motivation. *Psychological Review, 98*(2), 224–53.

Marshall, A. (1920). *Principles of Economics*. 8th edition. London: Macmillan.

Martin, R. (2012). Regional economic resilience, hysteresis and recessionary shocks. *Journal of Economic Geography, 12*(1), 1–32.

Martin, R., & Sunley, P. (2006). Path dependence and regional economic evolution. *Journal of Economic Geography, 6*, 395–437.

Martin, R., & Sunley, P. (2015). On the notion of regional economic resilience: conceptualisation and explanation. *Journal of Economic Geography, 15*(1), 1–42.

Marx, K. (1859). *Zur Kritik der Politischen Ökonomie. [A Critique of Political Economy]*. Berlin: Franz Duncker.

Masten, A. S., Desjardins, C. D., McCormick, C. M., Kuo, S. I. C., & Long, J. D. (2010). The significance of childhood competence and problems for adult success in work: a developmental cascade analysis. *Development and Psychopathology, 22*(3), 679–94.

Masterpasqua, F. (2009). Psychology and epigenetics. *Review of General Psychology, 13*(3), 194–201.

Matz, S. C., Appel, R. E., & Kosinski, M. (2020). Privacy in the age of psychological targeting. *Current Opinion in Psychology, 31*, 116–21.

Matz, S. C., Kosinski, M., Nave, G., & Stillwell, D. J. (2017). Psychological targeting as an effective approach to digital mass persuasion. *Proceedings of the National Academy of Sciences, 114*(48), 12714–19.

Maydeu-Olivares, A., Shi, D., & Fairchild, A. J. (2020). Estimating causal effects in linear regression models with observational data: the instrumental variables regression model. *Psychological Methods, 25*(2), 243–58.

Mazur, A., & Rosa, E. (1977). An empirical test of McClelland's "achieving society" theory. *Social Forces, 55*, 769–74.

McAdams, D. P., & Pals, J. L. (2006). A new Big Five: fundamental principles for an integrative science of personality. *American Psychologist, 61,* 204–17.

McCann, P., & Ortega-Argilés, R. (2016). Smart specialisation, entrepreneurship and SMEs: issues and challenges for a results-oriented EU regional policy. *Small Business Economics, 46*(4), 537–52.

McClelland, D. (1961). *The Achieving Society.* Princeton, NJ: Van Nostrand.

McClelland, D. C. (1965a). Achievement motivation can be developed. *Harvard Business Review, 43,* 6–25.

McClelland, D. C. (1965b). N achievement and entrepreneurship: a longitudinal study. *Journal of Personality and Social Psychology, 1*(4), 389–92.

McClelland, D. C. (1987). *Human Motivation.* New York: Cambridge University Press.

McCrae, R. R. (1996). Social consequences of experiential openness. *Psychological Bulletin, 120*(3), 323–37.

McCrae, R. R. (2001). Trait psychology and culture: exploring intercultural comparisons. *Journal of Personality, 69*(6), 819–46.

McCrae, R. R., & Costa, Jr., P. T. (2008). The five-factor theory of personality. In O. P. John, R. W. Robins, & L. A. Pervin (eds.), *Handbook of Personality: Theory and Research,* 3rd edition, 159–81. New York: Guilford Press.

McGranahan, D. A., & and Wojan, T. R. (2007). Recasting the creative class to examine growth processes in rural and urban counties. *Regional Studies, 41*(2), 197–216.

McMullen, J. S., Ingram, K. M., & Adams, J. (2020). What makes an entrepreneurship study entrepreneurial? Toward a unified theory of entrepreneurial agency. *Entrepreneurship Theory and Practice,* 10.1177/1042258720922460.

Miller, G. A., Galanter, E., & Pribram, K. H. (1960). *Plans and the Structure of Behavior.* London: Holt.

Minniti, M. (2005). Agglomeration and network externalities. *Journal of Economic Behavior & Organization, 57,* 1–27.

Miron, D., & McClelland, D. C. (1979). The effect of achievement motivation training on small business. *California Management Review, 21,* 13–28.

Mmbaga, N. A., Mathias, B. D., Williams, D. W., & Cardon, M. S. (2020). A review of and future agenda for research on identity in entrepreneurship. *Journal of Business Venturing, 35*(6), 106049. Available at https://www.sciencedirect.com/science/article/abs/pii/S0883902620306571.

Moffitt, T. E., Caspi, A., & Rutter, M. (2005). Strategy for investigating interactions between measured genes and measured environments. *Archives of General Psychiatry, 62*(5), 473–81.

Mueller, P. (2006). Entrepreneurship in the region: breeding ground for nascent entrepreneurs? *Small Business Economics, 27*(1), 41–58.

Mueller, P., Van Stel, A., & Storey, D. J. (2008). The effect of new firm formation on regional development over time: the case of Great Britain. *Small Business Economics, 30*, 59–71.

Murnieks, C. Y., Mosakowski, E., & Cardon, M. S. (2014). Pathways of passion: identity centrality, passion, and behavior among entrepreneurs. *Journal of Management, 40*(6), 1583–606.

Murray, H. G., Rushton, J. P., & Paunonen, S. V. (1990). Teacher personality traits and student instructional ratings in six types of university courses. *Journal of Educational Psychology, 82*(2), 250–61.

Nanda, R., & Sørenson, J. B. (2010). Workplace peers and entrepreneurship. *Management Science, 56*(7), 1116–26.

Nathan, M. (2015). After Florida: towards an economics of diversity. *European Urban and Regional Studies, 22*(1), 3–19.

Nathan, M., & Lee, N. (2013). Cultural diversity, innovation, and entrepreneurship: firm-level evidence from London. *Economic Geography, 89*(4), 367–94.

Naughton, M. J., & Cornwall, J. R. (2006). The virtue of courage in entrepreneurship: engaging the Catholic social tradition and the life-cycle of the business. *Business Ethics Quarterly, 16*, 69–93.

Newman, A., Obschonka, M., Moeller, J., & Chandan, G. G. (2021). Entrepreneurial passion: a review, synthesis, and agenda for future research. *Applied Psychology, 70*(2), 816–60. Available at https://doi.org/10.1111/apps.12236.

Newman, A., Obschonka, M., Schwarz, S., Cohen, M., & Nielsen, I. (2019). Entrepreneurial self-efficacy: a systematic review of the literature on its theoretical foundations, measurement, antecedents, and outcomes, and an agenda for future research. *Journal of Vocational Behavior, 110*, 403–19.

Nguyen, T. Q., Schmid, I., & Stuart, E. A. (2020). Clarifying causal mediation analysis for the applied researcher: defining effects based on what we want to learn. *Psychological Methods.* Available at https://doi.org/10.1037/met0000299.

Nicolaou, N., Shane, S., Cherkas, L., Hunkin, J., & Spector, T. D. (2008). Is the tendency to engage in entrepreneurship genetic? *Management Science, 54*(1), 167–79.

North, D. C. (1994). Economic performance through time. *American Economic Review*, *84*(3), 359–68.

Nunn, N. (2009). The importance of history for economic development. *Annual Review of Economics*, *1*, 65–92.

Nunn, N. (2012). Culture and the historical process. *Economic History of Developing Regions*, *27*(supp. 1), S108–S126.

Nunn, N., & Wantchekon, L. (2011). The slave trade and the origins of mistrust in Africa. *American Economic Review*, *101*(7), 3221–52.

Obradovich, N., Özak, Ö., Martín, I., Ortuño-Ortín, I., Awad, E., Cebrián, M., … & Cuevas, Á. (2020). *Expanding the Measurement of Culture with a Sample of Two Billion Humans* (No. w27827). Cambridge, MA: National Bureau of Economic Research.

Obschonka, M. (2016). Adolescent pathways to entrepreneurship. *Child Development Perspectives*, *10*(3), 196–201.

Obschonka, M. (2017). The quest for the entrepreneurial culture: psychological big data in entrepreneurship research. *Current Opinion in Behavioral Sciences*, *18*, 69–74.

Obschonka, M. (2018). The Industrial Revolution left psychological scars that can still be seen today. *Harvard Business Review*, 1–6. Available at https://hbr.org/2018/03/research-the-industrial-revolution-left-psychological-scars-that-can-still-be-seen-today.

Obschonka, M. (2019). Off to new shores: knowledge spillovers between economics and psychology or how I published with David Audretsch in *PLOS One*. In E. Lehmann & M. Keilbach (eds.), *From Industrial Organization to Entrepreneurship*, 425–9. Cham: Springer.

Obschonka, M., & Audretsch, D. B. (2020). Artificial intelligence and big data in entrepreneurship: a new era has begun. *Small Business Economics*, *55*(3), 529–39.

Obschonka, M., Hahn, E., & Bajwa, N. (2018). Personal agency in newly arrived refugees: the role of personality, entrepreneurial cognitions and intentions, and career adaptability. *Journal of Vocational Behavior*, *105*, 173–84.

Obschonka, M., Hakkarainen, K., Lonka, K., & Salmela-Aro, K. (2017). Entrepreneurship as a twenty-first century skill: entrepreneurial alertness and intention in the transition to adulthood. *Small Business Economics*, *48*(3), 487–501.

Obschonka, M., Kautonen, T., Ebert, T., & Goetz, F. (2020b). Harry Potter and the start-ups: fictional personality profiles predict entrepreneurship. *Academy of Management Proceedings*, *1*, 18483.

Obschonka, M., Lee, N., Rodríguez-Pose, A., Eichstaedt, J. C., & Ebert, T. (2020a). Big data methods, social media, and the psychology of entrepreneurial regions: capturing cross-county personality traits and their impact on entrepreneurship in the USA. *Small Business Economics*, *55*(3), 567–88.

Obschonka, M., Schmitt-Rodermund, E., Silbereisen, R. K., Gosling, S. D., & Potter, J. (2013). The regional distribution and correlates of an entrepreneurship-prone personality profile in the United States, Germany, and the United Kingdom: a socioecological perspective. *Journal of Personality and Social Psychology*, *105*(1), 104–22.

Obschonka, M., Silbereisen, R. K., & Schmitt-Rodermund, E. (2011b). Successful entrepreneurship as developmental outcome: a path model from a lifespan perspective of human development. *European Psychologist*, *16*(3), 174–86.

Obschonka, M., Silbereisen, R. K., Schmitt-Rodermund, E., & Stuetzer, M. (2011a). Nascent entrepreneurship and the developing individual: early entrepreneurial competence in adolescence and venture creation success during the career. *Journal of Vocational Behavior*, *79*(1), 121–33.

Obschonka, M., & Stuetzer, M. (2017). Integrating psychological approaches to entrepreneurship: the Entrepreneurial Personality System (EPS). *Small Business Economics*, *49*(1), 203–31.

Obschonka, M., Stuetzer, M., Audretsch, D. B., Rentfrow, P. J., Potter, J., & Gosling, S. D. (2016). Macropsychological factors predict regional economic resilience during a major economic crisis. *Social Psychological and Personality Science*, *7*(2), 95–104.

Obschonka, M., Stuetzer, M., Gosling, S. D., Rentfrow, P. J., Lamb, M. E., Potter, J., & Audretsch, D. B. (2015). Entrepreneurial regions: do macro-psychological cultural characteristics of regions help solve the "knowledge paradox" of economics? *PloS One*, *10*(6), e0129332.

Obschonka, M., Stuetzer, M., Rentfrow, P. J., Shaw-Taylor, L., Satchell, M., Silbereisen, R. K., Potter, J., & Gosling, S. D. (2018). In the shadow of coal: how large-scale industries contributed to present-day regional differences in personality and well-being. *Journal of Personality and Social Psychology*, *115*(5), 903–27.

Obschonka, M., Wyrwich, M., Fritsch, M., Gosling, S. D., Rentfrow, P. J., & Potter, J. (2019). Von unterkühlten Norddeutschen, gemütlichen Süddeutschen und aufgeschlossenen Großstädtern: Regionale Persönlichkeitsunterschiede in Deutschland [Reserved northerners, jovial southerners, and open urbanites: regional personality differences in Germany]. *Psychologische Rundschau*, *70*, 173–94.

O'Donnell, K. J., & Meaney, M. J. (2020). Epigenetics, development, and psychopathology. *Annual Review of Clinical Psychology, 16,* 327–50.

OECD (2020). *International Compendium of Entrepreneurship Policies,* OECD Studies on SMEs and Entrepreneurship. Paris: OECD Publishing. Available at https://doi.org/10.1787/338f1873 -en.

Oishi, S. (2014). Socioecological psychology. *Annual Review of Psychology, 65,* 581–609.

Oishi, S., & Graham, J. (2010). Social ecology: lost and found in psychological science. *Perspectives on Psychological Science, 5*(4), 356–77.

Olick, J. K. (1999). Collective memory: the two cultures. *Sociological Theory, 17*(3), 333–48.

Olick, J. K., Vinitzky-Seroussi, V., & Levy, D. (2011). Introduction. In J. K. Olick, V. Vinitzky-Seroussi, & D. Levy (eds.), *The Collective Memory Reader,* 3–62. Oxford: Oxford University Press.

Oosterbeek, H., Van Praag, M., & Ijsselstein, A. (2010). The impact of entrepreneurship education on entrepreneurship skills and motivation. *European Economic Review, 54*(3), 442–54.

Park, G., Schwartz, H. A., Eichstaedt, J. C., Kern, M. L., Kosinski, M., Stillwell, D. J.,Ungar, L. H., & Seligman, M. E. (2015). Automatic personality assessment through social media language. *Journal of Personality and Social Psychology, 108*(6), 934–52.

Parker, S. C. (2004). *The Economics of Self-employment and Entrepreneurship.* Cambridge: Cambridge University Press.

Parker, S. C. (2009). Why do small firms produce the entrepreneurs? *Journal of Socio-Economics, 38,* 484–94.

Pennebaker, J. W., Boyd, R. L., Jordan, K., & Blackburn, K. (2015). *The Development and Psychometric Properties of LIWC2015.* Austin, TX: University of Texas at Austin. Available at https:// www.researchgate.net/publication/282124505_The_Development _and_Psychometric_Properties_of_LIWC2015.

Peters, H., Götz, F. M., Ebert, T., Müller, S., Rentfrow, J., Gosling, S. D., & Matz, S. (2020). *Regional Personality Predicts the Early Spread of COVID-19 and Social Distancing Behavior.* Available at https://www.researchgate.net/publication/343482729 _Regional_Personality_Predicts_the_Early_Spread_of_COVID -19_and_Social_Distancing_Behavior.

Pickel, A. (1992). *Radical Transitions: The Survival and Revival of Entrepreneurship in the GDR.* Boulder, CO: Westview Press.

Plomin, R. E., DeFries, J. C., Craig, I. W., & McGuffin, P. E. (eds.) (2003). *Behavioral Genetics in the Postgenomic Era*. Washington, DC: American Psychological Association.

Putnam, R. D. (2000). *Bowling Alone: The Collapse and Revival of American Community*. New York: Simon & Schuster.

Quality Assurance Agency [QAA] (2012). Enterprise and entrepreneurship education: guidance for UK higher education providers. Available at https://www.qaa.ac.uk/docs/qaas/enhancement-and-development/enterprise-and-entrpreneurship-education-2018.pdf?sfvrsn=15f1f981_8.

Ramoglou, S., Gartner, W. B., & Tsang, E. W. (2020). "Who is an entrepreneur?" is (still) the wrong question. *Journal of Business Venturing Insights*, *13*, e00168.

Rate, C. R. (2010). Defining the features of courage: a search for meaning. In C. L. S. Pury & S. J. Lopez (eds.), *The Psychology of Courage: Modern Research on an Ancient Virtue*, 47–66. Washington, DC: American Psychological Association.

Rauch, A., & Frese, M. (2007). Let's put the person back into entrepreneurship research: a meta-analysis on the relationship between business owners' personality traits, business creation, and success. *European Journal of Work and Organizational Psychology*, *16*(4), 353–85.

Rentfrow, P. J. (2020). Geographical psychology. *Current Opinion in Psychology*, *32*, 165–70.

Rentfrow, P. J., Gosling, S. D., & Potter, J. (2008). A theory of the emergence, persistence, and expression of geographic variation in psychological characteristics. *Perspectives on Psychological Science*, *3*(5), 339–69.

Rentfrow, P. J., & Jokela, M. (2016). Geographical psychology: the spatial organization of psychological phenomena. *Current Directions in Psychological Science*, *25*(6), 393–8.

Roberts, B. W. (2018). A revised sociogenomic model of personality traits. *Journal of Personality*, *86*(1), 23–35.

Roberts, B. W., Caspi, A., & Moffitt, T. E. (2003). Work experiences and personality development in young adulthood. *Journal of Personality and Social Psychology*, *84*(3), 582–93.

Roberts, B. W., & DelVecchio, W. F. (2000). The rank-order consistency of personality traits from childhood to old age: a quantitative review of longitudinal studies. *Psychological Bulletin*, *126*(1), 3–25.

Roberts, B. W., & Mroczek, D. (2008). Personality trait change in adulthood. *Current Directions in Psychological Science*, *17*(1), 31–5.

Robinson, W. (1950). Ecological correlations and the behavior of individuals. *American Sociological Review*, *15*, 351–7.

Roediger, H. L., & DeSoto, K. A. (2014). Forgetting the presidents. *Science*, *346*(6213), 1106–9.

Rozin, P. (2003). Five potential principles for understanding cultural differences in relation to individual differences. *Journal of Research in Personality*, *37*, 273–83.

Runco, M. A. (2004). Everyone has creative potential. In R. J. Sternberg, E. L. Grigorenko, & J. L. Singer (eds.), *Creativity: From Potential to Realization*, 21–30. Washington, DC: American Psychological Association.

Ruskovaara, E., & Pihkala, T. (2015). Entrepreneurship education in schools: empirical evidence on the teacher's role. *The Journal of Educational Research*, *108*(3), 236–49.

Rutter, M. (2006). *Genes and Behavior: Nature–Nurture Interplay Explained*. Oxford: Blackwell Publishing.

Ryff, C. D. (2019). Entrepreneurship and eudaimonic well-being: five venues for new science. *Journal of Business Venturing*, *34*(4), 646–63.

Savickas, M. L. (2002). Career construction: a developmental theory of vocational behavior. In D. Brown (ed.), *Career Choice and Development*, 4th edition, 149–205. San Francisco, CA: Jossey-Bass.

Saxenian, A. (1996). *Regional Advantage*. Cambridge, MA: Harvard University Press.

Saxenian, A. (1999). *Silicon Valley's New Immigrant Entrepreneurs*. San Francisco: Public Policy Institute of California.

Schatz, S. P. (1965). Achievement and economic growth: a critique. *The Quarterly Journal of Economics*, *79*, 234–45.

Schindele, Y., & Weyh, A. (2011). The direct employment effects of new businesses in Germany revisited—an empirical investigation for 1976–2004. *Small Business Economics*, *36*, 353–63.

Schmitt-Rodermund, E. (2004). Pathways to successful entrepreneurship: parenting, personality, entrepreneurial competence, and interests. *Journal of Vocational Behavior*, *65*, 498–518.

Schmitt-Rodermund, E. (2007). The long way to entrepreneurship: personality, parenting, early interests, and competencies as precursors for entrepreneurial activity among the "Termites". In R. K. Silbereisen & R. M. Lerner (eds.), *Approaches to Positive Youth Development*, 205–24. London: Sage Publications.

Schmitt-Rodermund, E., Schröder, E., & Obschonka, M. (2019). Studying entrepreneurial occupations in the Terman women. *International Journal of Psychology*, *54*(2), 164–73.

Schneider, B., Goldstiein, H. W., & Smith, D. B. (1995). The ASA framework: an update. *Personnel Psychology*, *48*(4), 747–73. Available at https://onlinelibrary.wiley.com/doi/abs/10.1111/j .1744-6570.1995.tb01780.x.

Schoon, I., & Duckworth, K. (2012). Who becomes an entrepreneur? Early life experiences as predictors of entrepreneurship. *Developmental Psychology*, *48*(6), 1719–26.

Schröder, E., & Schmitt-Rodermund, E. (2006). Crystallizing enterprising interests among adolescents through a career development program: the role of personality and family background. *Journal of Vocational Behavior*, *69*(3), 494–509.

Schulz, J. F., Bahrami-Rad, D., Beauchamp, J. P., & Henrich, J. (2019). The Church, intensive kinship, and global psychological variation. *Science*, *366*(6466). Available at https://science .sciencemag.org/content/366/6466/eaau5141.

Schumpeter, J. A. (1934). *The Theory of Economic Development*. Cambridge, MA: Havard University Press.

Schwab, A., & Zhang, Z. A. (2018). New methodological frontier in entrepreneurship research: big data studies. *Entrepreneurship Theory and Practice*, *43*(5), 843–54.

Schwartz, S. H. (1994). Beyond individualism/collectivism: new cultural dimensions of values. In U. Kim, H. C. Triandis, C. Kagitcibasi, S.-C. Choi, & G. Yoon (eds.), *Individualism and Collectivism: Theory, Method, and Applications*, 85–119. Thousand Oaks, CA: Sage Publications.

Segall, M. H., Lonner, W. J., & Berry, J. W. (1998). Cross-cultural psychology as a scholarly discipline: on the flowering of culture in behavioral research. *American Psychologist*, *53*(10), 1101–10.

Seikkula-Leino, J., Ruskovaara, E., Ikavalko, M., Mattila, J., & Rytkola, T. (2010). Promoting entrepreneurship education: the role of the teacher? *Education and Training*, *52*(2), 117–27.

Selby, E. C., Shaw, E. J., & Houtz, J. C. (2005). The creative personality. *Gifted Child Quarterly*, *49*(4), 300–314.

Semrad, A. (2015). Education, immigration, and economic development: evidence from 19th and 20th century Bavaria. PhD dissertation, Ludwig-Maximilians Universität, München.

Shane, S. A. (1992). Why do some societies invent more than others? *Journal of Business Venturing*, *7*(1), 29–46.

Shane, S., Locke, E. A., & Collins, C. J. (2003). Entrepreneurial motivation. *Human Resource Management Review*, *13*(2), 257–79.

Shane, S., Nicolaou, N., Cherkas, L., & Spector, T. D. (2010). Genetics, the Big Five, and the tendency to be self-employed. *Journal of Applied Psychology*, *95*(6), 1154–62.

Sheldon, K. M., & Kasser, T. (1995). Coherence and congruence: two aspects of personality integration. *Journal of Personality and Social Psychology*, *68*(3), 531–43.

Shepherd, D. A. (2003). Learning from business failure: propositions of grief recovery for the self-employed. *Academy of Management Review*, *28*(2), 318–28.

Shepherd, D. A. (2004). Educating entrepreneurship students about emotion and learning from failure. *Academy of Management Learning & Education*, *3*(3), 274–87.

Shepherd, D. A. (2015). Party on! A call for entrepreneurship research that is more interactive, activity based, cognitively hot, compassionate, and prosocial. *Journal of Business Venturing*, *30*(4), 489–507.

Shepherd, D. A., Covin, J. G., & Kuratko, D. F. (2009). Project failure from corporate entrepreneurship: managing the grief process. *Journal of Business Venturing*, *24*(6), 588–600.

Shepherd, D. A., Saade, F. P., & Wincent, J. (2020). How to circumvent adversity? Refugee-entrepreneurs' resilience in the face of substantial and persistent adversity. *Journal of Business Venturing*, *35*(4), 105940.

Shepherd, D. A., & Suddaby, R. (2017). Theory building: a review and integration. *Journal of Management*, *43*(1), 59–86.

Shepherd, D. A., & Williams, T. A. (2014). Local venturing as compassion organizing in the aftermath of a natural disaster: the role of localness and community in reducing suffering. *Journal of Management Studies*, *51*(6), 952–94.

Shepherd, D. A., & Williams, T. A. (2018). *Spontaneous Venturing: An Entrepreneurial Approach to Alleviating Suffering in the Aftermath of a Disaster*. Cambridge, MA: MIT Press.

Simon, H. A. (1991). Bounded rationality and organizational learning. *Organization Science*, *2*(1), 125–34.

Snijders, T. A. B., & Bosker, R. J. (1999). *Multilevel Analysis: An Introduction to Basic and Advanced Multilevel Modeling*. London: Sage Publications.

Sorenson, O., & Audia, P. G. (2000). The social structure of entrepreneurial activity: geographic concentration of footwear production in the United States, 1940–1989. *American Journal of Sociology*, *106*, 424–62.

Specht, J., Bleidorn, W., Denissen, J. J., Hennecke, M., Hutteman, R., Kandler, C., Luhmann, M., Orth, U., Reitz, A. K., & Zimmermann, J. (2014). What drives adult personality development? A comparison of theoretical perspectives and empirical evidence. *European Journal of Personality*, *28*(3), 216–30.

Specht, J., Egloff, B., & Schmukle, S. C. (2011). Stability and change of personality across the life course: the impact of age and major life events on mean-level and rank-order stability of the Big Five. *Journal of Personality and Social Psychology, 101*(4), 862–82.

Stam, E. (2015). Entrepreneurial ecosystems and regional policy: a sympathetic critique. *European Planning Studies, 23*(9), 1759–69.

Steel, P., Taras, V., Uggerslev, K., & Bosco, F. (2018). The happy culture: a theoretical, meta-analytic, and empirical review of the relationship between culture and wealth and subjective well-being. *Personality and Social Psychology Review, 22*(2), 128–69.

Stephan, U. (2018). Entrepreneurs' mental health and well-being: a review and research agenda. *Academy of Management Perspectives, 32*(3), 290–322.

Stephan, U., & Pathak, S. (2016). Beyond cultural values? Cultural leadership ideals and entrepreneurship. *Journal of Business Venturing, 31*(5), 505–23.

Stephan, U., Tavares, S. M., Carvalho, H., Ramalho, J. J., Santos, S. C., & van Veldhoven, M. (2020). Self-employment and eudaimonic well-being: energized by meaning, enabled by societal legitimacy. *Journal of Business Venturing, 35*(6), 106047. Available at doi.org/10.1016/j.jbusvent.2020.106047.

Stephan, U., & Uhlaner, L. M. (2010). Performance-based vs socially supportive culture: a cross-national study of descriptive norms and entrepreneurship. *Journal of International Business Studies, 41*(8), 1347–64.

Sternberg, R. (2009). Regional dimensions of entrepreneurship. *Foundations and Trends® in Entrepreneurship, 5*(4), 211–340.

Sternberg, R. J., & Lubart, T. I. (1996). Investing in creativity. *American Psychologist, 57*(1), 677–88.

Stewart, W. H., & Roth, P. L. (2007). A meta-analysis of achievement motivation differences between entrepreneurs and managers. *Journal of Small Business Management, 45*(4), 401–21.

Stigler, S. M. (1981). Gauss and the invention of least squares. *The Annals of Statistics, 9*(3), 465–74.

Stiglitz, J. (2010). *Freefall: America, Free Markets, and the Sinking of the World Economy.* New York: W. W. Norton & Company.

Stuetzer, M., Audretsch, D. B., Obschonka, M., Gosling, S. D., Rentfrow, P. J., & Potter, J. (2018). Entrepreneurship culture, knowledge spillovers, and the growth of regions. *Regional Studies, 52*(5), 608–18.

Stuetzer, M., Obschonka, M., Audretsch, D. B., Wyrwich, M., Rentfrow, P. J., Coombes, M., Shaw-Taylor, L., & Satchell,

M. (2016). Industry structure, entrepreneurship, and culture: an empirical analysis using historical coalfields. *European Economic Review*, *86*, 52–72.

Suddaby, R. (2014). Why theory? *Academy of Management Review*, *39*(4), 407–11.

Suddle, K., Beugelsdijk, S., & Wennekers, S. (2010). Entrepreneurial culture and its effect on the rate of nascent entrepreneurship. In A. Freytag & R. Thurik (eds.), *Entrepreneurship and Culture*, 227–44. Heidelberg, Dordrecht, London, New York: Springer.

Super, D. E. (1963). Self-concepts in vocational development. In D. E. Super, R. Starishevsky, N. Matlin, & J. P. Joordan (eds.), *Career Development: Self-Concept Theory*, 17–32. New York: College Entrance Examination Board.

Sylwester, K., & Purver, M. (2015). Twitter language use reflects psychological differences between democrats and republicans. *PloS One*, *10*(9), e0137422.

Tabellini, G. (2010). Culture and institutions: economic development in the regions of Europe. *Journal of the European Economic Association*, *8*(4), 677–716.

Tajfel, H. (ed.) (2010). *Social Identity and Intergroup Relations*, Vol. 7. Cambridge: Cambridge University Press.

Talhelm, T., Zhang, X., Oishi, S., Shimin, C., Duan, D., Lan, X., & Kitayama, S. (2014). Large-scale psychological differences within China explained by rice versus wheat agriculture. *Science*, *344*(6184), 603–8.

Taylor, S. E., Sherman, D. K., Kim, H. S., Jarcho, J., Takagi, K., & Dunagan, M. S. (2004). Culture and social support: who seeks it and why? *Journal of Personality and Social Psychology*, *87*(3), 354–62. Available at https://psycnet.apa.org/record/2004-18348-006.

The New York Times (2020). "The Social Dilemma" review: unplug and run. Available at https://www.nytimes.com/2020/09/09/movies/the-social-dilemma-review.html.

Thomas, M. (1996). How to become an entrepreneur in East Germany: conditions, steps and effects of the constitution of new entrepreneurs. In H. Brezinski & M. Fritsch (eds.), *The Economic Impact of New Firms in Post-Socialist Countries—Bottom Up Transformation in Eastern Europe*, 227–32. Cheltenham, UK and Brookfield, VT, USA: Edward Elgar Publishing.

Tourish, D. (2019). The triumph of nonsense in management studies. *Academy of Management Learning & Education*, *19*(1), 99–109.

Tversky, A., & Kahneman, D. (1974). Judgment under uncertainty: heuristics and biases. *Science*, *185*(4157), 1124–30.

Ullen, F., Hambrick, D. Z., & Mosing, M. A. (2016). Rethinking expertise: a multifactorial gene–environment interaction model of expert performance. *Psychological Bulletin, 142*(4), 427–46. Available at https://scottbarrykaufman.com/wp-content/uploads/2016/03/Ullen2015PsycholBull.pdf.

Usami, S., Murayama, K., & Hamaker, E. L. (2019). A unified framework of longitudinal models to examine reciprocal relations. *Psychological Methods, 24*(5), 637–57. Available at https://psycnet.apa.org/fulltext/2019-21491-001.html.

Van de Ven, A. H., & Johnson, P. E. (2006). Knowledge for theory and practice. *Academy of Management Review, 31*(4), 802–21.

Van Stel, A., & Suddle, K. (2008). The impact of new firm formation on regional development in the Netherlands. *Small Business Economics, 30*, 31–47.

Varian, H. R. (2016). Causal inference in economics and marketing. *Proceedings of the National Academy of Sciences, 113*(27), 7310–15.

Venkataraman, S. (2019). The distinctive domain of entrepreneurship research. In J. A. Katz & A. C. Corbet (eds.), *Seminal Ideas for the Next Twenty-Five Years of Advances* (Advances in Entrepreneurship, Firm Emergence and Growth, Vol. 21), 5–20. Bingley: Emerald Publishing.

Vinokur, A., & Caplan, R. D. (1987). Attitudes and social support: determinants of job-seeking behavior and well-being among the unemployed. *Journal of Applied Social Psychology, 17*(12), 1007–24.

Voigtländer, N., & Voth, H.-J. (2012). Persecution perpetuated: the medieval origins of anti-Semitic violence in Nazi Germany. *Quarterly Journal of Economics, 127*(3), 1339–92.

Wagner, J. (2004). Are young and small firms hothouses for nascent entrepreneurs? Evidence from German micro data. *Applied Economics Quarterly, 50*(4), 379–91.

Wei, W., et al. (2017). Regional ambient temperature is associated with human personality. *Nature Human Behaviour, 1*(12), 890–95.

Weick, K. E. (1995). What theory is not, theorizing is. *Administrative Science Quarterly, 40*(3), 385–90.

Welter, F. (2011). Contextualizing entrepreneurship: conceptual challenges and ways forward. *Entrepreneurship Theory and Practice, 35*(1), 165–84.

Welter, F., & Baker, T. (2020). Moving contexts onto new roads: clues from other disciplines. *Entrepreneurship in Theory and Practice.* Available at https://doi.org/10.1177/1042258720930996.

Welter, F., Baker, T., Audretsch, D. B., & Gartner, W. B. (2017). Everyday entrepreneurship: a call for entrepreneurship research to embrace entrepreneurial diversity. *Entrepreneurship in Theory & Practice*, *41*(3), 311–21.

Welter, F., & Gartner, W. B. (eds.) (2016). *A Research Agenda for Entrepreneurship and Context*. Cheltenham, UK and Northampton, MA, USA: Edward Elgar Publishing.

Westlund, H., & Bolton, R.E. (2003). Local social capital and entrepreneurship. *Small Business Economics*, *21*(2), 77–113.

Westlund, H., Larsson, J. P., & Olsson, A. R. (2014). Start-ups and local entrepreneurial social capital in the municipalities of Sweden. *Regional Studies*, *48*(6), 974–94.

Wigfield, A., Eccles, J. S., Fredricks, J. A., Simpkins, S., Roeser, R. W., & Schiefele, U. (2015). Development of achievement motivation and engagement. In R. Lerner (series ed.), & C. Garcia Coll & M. Lamb (volume eds.), *Handbook of Child Psychology*, 7th edition, *Vol. 3, Social and Emotional Development*, 657–700. New York: Wiley.

Wiklund, J., Hatak, I., Lerner, D. A., Verheul, I., Thurik, R., & Antshel, K. (2020). Entrepreneurship, clinical psychology, and mental health: an exciting and promising new field of research. *Academy of Management Perspectives*, *34*(2), 291–5.

Wiklund, J., Nikolaev, B., Shir, N., Foo, M. D., & Bradley, S. (2019). Entrepreneurship and well-being: past, present, and future. *Journal of Business Venturing*, *34*(4), 579–88.

Wiklund, J., Wright, M., & Zahra, S. A. (2019). Conquering relevance: entrepreneurship research's grand challenge. *Entrepreneurship: Theory and Practice*, *43*(3), 419–36.

Williams, N., & Vorley, T. (2014). Economic resilience and entrepreneurship: lessons from the Sheffield city region. *Entrepreneurship & Regional Development*, *26*(3–4), 257–81.

Williamson, O. E. (2000). The new institutional economics: taking stock, looking ahead. *Journal of Economic Literature*, *38*(3), 595–613.

Wilson, D. S., Hayes, S. C., Biglan, A., & Embry, D. D. (2014). Evolving the future: toward a science of intentional change. *The Behavioral and Brain Sciences*, *37*(4), 395–416.

Wincent, J., & Örtqvist, D. (2009). A comprehensive model of entrepreneur role stress antecedents and consequences. *Journal of Business and Psychology*, *24*(2), 225–43.

Wundt, W. (1874). *Grundzüge der physiologischen Psychologie* [*Principles of Physiological Psychology*]. Leipzig: Engelmann.

Wyrwich, M., Sternberg, R., & Stuetzer, M. (2019). Failing role models and the formation of fear of entrepreneurial failure: a study of regional peer effects in German regions. *Journal of Economic Geography*, *19*(3), 567–88.

Wyrwich, M., Stuetzer, M., & Sternberg, R. (2016). Entrepreneurial role models, fear of failure, and institutional approval of entrepreneurship: a tale of two regions. *Small Business Economics*, *46*(3), 467–92.

Zacher, H., & Frese, M. (2018). Action regulation theory: foundations, current knowledge and future directions. In D. S. Ones, N. Anderson, C. Viswesvaran, & H. K. Sinangil (eds.), *The SAGE Handbook of Industrial, Work & Organizational Psychology: Organizational Psychology*, 122–44. London: Sage Reference.

Zacher, H., Hacker, W., & Frese, M. (2016). Action regulation across the adult lifespan (ARAL): a metatheory of work and aging. *Work, Aging and Retirement*, *2*(3), 286–306.

Zhang, T. Y., & Meaney, M. J. (2010). Epigenetics and the environmental regulation of the genome and its function. *Annual Review of Psychology*, *61*, 439–66.

Zhao, H., & Seibert, S. E. (2006). The Big Five personality dimensions and entrepreneurial status: a meta-analytical review. *Journal of Applied Psychology*, *91*(2), 259–71.

Zhou, M., Zhou, Y., Zhang, J., Obschonka, M., & Silbereisen, R. K. (2019). Person–city personality fit and entrepreneurial success: an explorative study in China. *International Journal of Psychology*, *54*(2), 155–63.